Applying

W9-AOT-919

Adobe®
After Effects™

Studio Techniques

ROD HARLAN

SAMS

Sams Publishing

201 West 103rd Street,
Indianapolis, Indiana 46290

Applying Adobe After Effects Studio Techniques

International Standard Book Number: 0-672-31856-3

Library of Congress Catalog Card Number: 00-109547

Printed in the United States of America

First Printing: December 2000

03   02   01   00   4   3   2   1

ii

Trademarks

Warning and Disclaimer

Executive Editors
Jeff Schultz
Randi Roger

Development Editor
Jonathan Steever

Managing Editor
Charlotte Clapp

Project Editor
Carol Bowers

Copy Editor
Sean Medlock

Indexer
Chris Barrick

Proofreader
Tony Reitz

Technical Editor
Beth Roy

Team Coordinator
Amy Patton

Media Developer
JG Moore
Jason Haines

Interior Designer
Gary Adair

Cover Designer
Gary Adair

Production
Cheryl Lynch

Table of Contents

Contents

IX Evolution Effects

About the Author

Rod Harlan is Executive Director of the Digital Video Professionals Association (DVPA), the premiere organization of New Media enthusiasts devoted to promoting the growth, quality, and education of the digital video professional. As the Multimedia Editor for *Mac Design*, a print magazine for graphic designers using Macintosh computers, he regularly reviews and beta-tests many of the hottest hardware and software products before they're available to the mass market.

Harlan is the author of the "Digital Video View" and "DV News" columns in *Mac Design* and the "DV Workshop" column in *Photoshop User* magazine, and is the coauthor of *Adobe Web Design and Publishing Unleashed*, published by Sams. He's on the Advisory Council of the National Association of Photoshop Professionals (NAPP) and has also designed and produced the *Adobe After Effects: Professional Techniques* tutorial videotape for KW Computer Training.

Harlan is a frequent speaker and trainer at many of the largest conferences and expos on multimedia products and services, including MacWorld, NAB, DCC, Showbiz, and PhotoshopWorld. He's been involved with computer graphics since 1983 and works with all things related to digital video, including digital editing, animation, and special effects for television, video, CD-ROM, DVD, and the Internet.

For more background information, please visit **http://www.RodHarlan.com**.

Dedication

This book is dedicated to Katie Harlan, my mother, who passed away on Christmas morning and passed on to me the belief that all things are possible through prayer.

Acknowledgements

This book would not have been possible without the enormous effort put forth by so many talented people.

I'd like to thank Dean Harlan, my father, for always being encouraging and supportive... even when I take on more responsibility than I will ever have time to handle. I love you and appreciate all your help handling many of my responsibilities so I could finish this book. God blessed me by allowing me to be your son.

I'd like to thank my best friend and assistant extraordinaire Julie Otto for her endless hours of help and motivation throughout this project. You juggled the roles of proofreader, production coordinator, graphics manager, motivator, counselor, and advisor without ever complaining once. I appreciate you more than you'll ever know.

I'd like to thank Michael Barclay, who not only created the eye-catching 3D artwork in this volume, but who also designed and helped write many of the more in-depth chapters. His first love is 3D, as shown by his focus on depth and the interplay between layers in After Effects. Like many in our field, Michael learned AE mostly on his own, through trial and error, while trying to please his boss and exceed his clients' wishes. And like many in the compositing world, he felt that there was a need for a book that showed readers how to use AE out of the box to create real, money-making projects. (Although he was often heard to say that he missed using many of his favorite third-party plug-ins while working on these chapters.) I hope to find space for more of Michael's work in a future volume.

I'd like to thank Beth Roy for being the best tech editor I could have ever hoped for. Beth, your ideas always made the project better. Your suggestions always made the steps easier. Your explanations always made the techniques clearer. I hope I never have to do another book without you.

I'd like to thank the phenomenal community of my peers that I've met through the Digital Video Professionals Association (DVPA). Your ideas and feedback are the foundation for this book. Thanks to all who participated in the online surveys and help shape the design, layout, and special features in this book. Without your approval and support, this book would not have been published. I hope I've been able to include everyone's favorite features the way that you originally suggested them to me.

I'd like to thank my friends at KW Media Group, home of *Mac Design* and *Photoshop User* magazines, for always inspiring me to do better work. Special thanks go to Scott Kelby, for being a great mentor while showing me that business can be conducted with honor, and Chris Main, for always covering for me when I turned in every article and review late while writing this book.

I'd like to thank all of the wonderful staff at Macmillan, including Randi Roger, Jeff Schultz, Jon Steever, Carol Bowers, Sean Medlock, Mary Beth Wakefield, Jason Haines, J.G. Moore, Katie Robinson, Susan Hobbs, and many others who I never even met. Thank you for putting up with me when I got grumpy and frustrated with the slow pace and missteps this book took in the beginning, all while looking for ways to make it even better.

A big thank you goes to Steve Kilisky, senior product manager for Adobe After Effects, for spearheading the development of such a great product. Thank you for always making yourself available to me, answering all my questions, and buying me lunch on Adobe's dime.

I'd like to thank my good friend Ron Lindeboom, founder of the World Wide Users Groups (WWUG), for always providing encouragement when I need it most. We've both been working in the field of digital video since the beginning, and I can't think of anyone I'd rather explore new technology with.

I'd like to thank my friends Chad Anderson, Larry Sprinkle, Jason Lazzaro, Bill Greenwald, April Norris, Sarah Miller, Kerry Hillary, Nancy Jukes, and Thalia for putting up with months of me saying, "I swear the book is almost done. I'll have time when the book is done."

But mostly, I'd like to thank Jesus for giving me the strength to persevere in this ever-changing world of technology. Without his peace in these troubled times, I would have dropped out long ago.

Tell Us What You Think

As the reader of this book, *you* are the most important critic and commentator. We value your opinion and want to know what we're doing right, what we could do better, what areas you'd like to see us publish in, and any other words of wisdom you're willing to pass our way.

You can e-mail or write me directly to let me know what you did or didn't like about this book—as well as what we can do to make our books stronger.

Please note that I cannot help you with technical problems related to the topic of this book, and due to the high volume of mail I receive, I might not be able to reply to every message.

When you write, please be sure to include this book's title and author as well as your name and phone or fax number. I will carefully review your comments and share them with the author and editors who worked on the book.

E-mail: graphics_sams@mcp.com

Mail: Mark Taber
              Associate Publisher
              Sams Publishing
              201 West 103rd Street
              Indianapolis, Indiana 46290 USA

Introduction

In college, I participated in an alternative learning program called Interdisciplinary Studies (IDS). The IDS Program takes an integrated approach to teaching literature, history, philosophy, ethics, fine arts, and the social sciences, rather than teaching these disciplines as separate courses. One of the special features of the IDS Program is that it takes a group of students and a small team of instructors and sequesters them in their own building for two years, where they cover all of the core curriculum classes expected of freshmen and sophomores in college. The idea is to develop a learning community for the students and faculty in the program.

The interesting part about the program was how the students were actually taught. Instead of running around campus taking separate classes in writing, literature, philosophy, history, science, and so on, the participants in the IDS program would look at a period in history—say, ancient Greece—and learn everything we could about that time. We read all the Greek tragedies, learned from their philosophers, discovered their history, analyzed their technological and scientific achievements, and wrote about their accomplishments before moving on to another era—say, ancient Rome. Instead of taking separate classes and then figuring out how it all came together, my fellow students and I learned in a more streamlined fashion.

That experience has stayed with me and is the foundation for *Applying Adobe After Effects Studio Techniques*. This book has been written as concisely as possible without sacrificing the necessary insight and hands-on exercises you need to understand this complex software package. Each chapter is its own project, complete and self-contained. There's no need to start at the beginning of the book and read until the end. Instead, simply find the chapter that has the technique or effect that you want to learn, start at step 1, work through all the steps, and click Render. Voilà!

Who This Book Is For

Applying Adobe After Effects Studio Techniques is for the digital video artist who asks, "I saw this neat effect on TV. How do I do that?" Each chapter covers a specific technique and shows the appropriate screen shot for each step. It not only shows *how* to use the technique, but *when*. And each chapter is independent of the rest so that you can zero in on each specific technique. This book is intended for everyone, from beginners who have never animated a single object to intermediate-level motion graphic artists who want to add a few more techniques to their arsenal.

This book was also written with both Macintosh and Windows users in mind. Because After Effects is immensely popular on both platforms, I went to great lengths to make this book the ultimate resource on cross-platform compatibility for After Effects users. Unlike many other books, *Applying Adobe After Effects Studio Techniques* has screen shots from both the Mac and PC versions of After Effects. More importantly, every keyboard shortcut is given with both the Macintosh and Windows equivalent.

How to Use This Book

First of all, this book is meant to be *used*. Fold it, bend it, draw doodles in it, and write notes in the margins. It should become your workbook for After Effects. It definitely should *not* be a leisurely read while you're sitting in your recliner sipping a glass of your favorite wine. Instead, prop it up next to your computer and start diving into the techniques!

How This Book is Set Up

Although this book walks you through setting up a project in After Effects, the focus is on learning the software quickly. If you're a beginner, you'll be able to create sophisticated effects while learning the software. If you're an accomplished artist, you'll be able to quickly learn some of the most popular techniques used in television and film today.

The projects and artwork files in this book were all created at a size of 320×240 pixels. Obviously, broadcast television and film use a much higher resolution. However, I wanted to make sure that you can access the files on the CD and build the projects in all of the chapters, whether you're in a large studio on a multiprocessor workstation or in a cramped airplane seat working on a laptop. Working at this smaller size requires less disk space, processor power, and RAM.

All of the final rendered movies are saved using either the Sorenson or Animation codec. These compression standards make it easy to play the files directly off the CD, or you can conserve disk space after you've completed a chapter and you're saving your work to disk. Obviously, if you're planning to use one of the techniques for TV, DVD, video, or film (instead of just for practice), you'll want to save it to the appropriate file format for your project.

This book is set up in a non-linear manner, just like After Effects. You can turn to any chapter in the book and complete it without having to refer to any other section of the book. All of the tips, tricks, techniques, and explanations are right in front of you, where you need them most.

What This Book Assumes

This book assumes that you want to make money by working with Adobe After Effects. It also assumes that you want to have a good time while you're making that money. However, if you're looking for a replacement for the After Effects manual, you've come to the wrong place. You won't find long explanations of every possible menu selection, nor are there any deep analyses of how this application came to exist. Instead, you'll find tips, tricks, and shortcuts to make your After Effects experience the best it can be.

How This Book Is Organized

Section I—Transfer Modes

Section I will show you how to transfer files from Adobe Photoshop, Adobe Illustrator, and Adobe Premiere into After Effects. You'll learn how to best prepare your files before exporting them to After Effects, and what to do when things don't go exactly as planned. You'll also learn how to work backwards in time, copy settings between layers, relink lost media files, create seamlessly looping scenery, animate layers from other programs, replace effects that won't import from other programs, and much more.

Section II—Text and Number Effects

Most After Effects projects use text and numbers to communicate their message. This section will show you how to create floating text on water, make text follow a complicated path, create an animated signature, and create a animated numerical gauge. You'll also learn how to apply displacement maps, create a path with the pen tool, work with open and closed masks, add blurs, glows, and drop shadows, understand linear acceleration graphs, and change velocity controls, among other techniques.

Section III—Web Effects

Although this is the shortest section in the book, it's also one of the most relevant. In this section, you'll learn how to create an animated Web banner. In the process, you'll set and animate the positions of Photoshop layers, set Color Palette, Transparency, Dithering, and Looping options, save to the animated GIF format directly from After Effects, export still images to make file sizes even smaller, and present a call to action in a Web banner to generate the most clickthrough traffic.

Section IV—Video Effects

This section will look at a few down-and-dirty video effects that are popular today, including giving animation a handheld camcorder look and creating promos quickly and easily. You'll learn how to use special After Effects features like the Wiggler and the Smoother. You'll also learn about controlling chaos, lessening your rendering time, reversing video, and the best keyboard shortcut in all of After Effects.

Section V—Background Effects

It's fine to use a still photo as a background plate for an animated sequence, but it's even better when you can bring that still photo to life. In this section, you'll make a waving flag from a still photo using the Displacement Map effect. Specifically, you'll learn how to apply a displacement to just a portion of the image, create a mask, pre-compose a layer, and use Mask Feather.

Section VI—Particle Playground Effects

Section VI will teach you about the advanced features found in Particle Playground. You'll learn how to make blood drip from the text "Happy Halloween" by using the Pen tool to draw a mask, animating a Producer Point, creating a Ramp, and then applying a track matte to that Ramp.

Section VII—Motion Math Effects

Motion Math is another area of After Effects that gives many users pause. In this section, you'll use it with an audio clip to animate a graphic file. You'll also apply stock video/animation as a texture, assign transparency modes, create alpha mattes, animate a logo to the beat of the music, and learn about the Comp Audio script.

Section VIII—Miscellaneous Effects

As the title implies, this is a catch-all section of the book. This section will show you how to create an animated jigsaw puzzle, an opening iris, an animated station ID, and even a smoky haze, all without having to buy an expensive plug-in. You'll also learn how to slice an image into pieces, use color keys and matte chokers, rotate layers on their anchor points, loop imported footage, keyframe opacity for a fluid look, and animate the amount of displacement that takes place in a composition.

Section IX—Evolution Effects

Multiplane, one of the free plug-ins bundled with this book, comes from the Atomic Power Evolution plug-in package. This plug-in allows you to place your After Effects layers in a 3D space. In this section, you'll learn how to install third-party plug-ins, import Illustrator files for use with Multiplane, fix gradients imported from Illustrator, set up layers in 3D space, cast shadows correctly in 3D space, animate camera position in 3D space, and much more.

What's on the CD-ROMs?

On the first CD-ROM, you'll find a folder for each chapter with all of the artwork you need to re-create that technique. All of the files are organized by chapter number. You'll also find a Final Movie folder with a QuickTime clip of what your final rendered project for that chapter should look like. Feel free to play this clip before you start the chapter so that you know exactly what you're building. After you finish the chapter, it's also a good idea to compare this clip to your rendered movie to see if there are any discrepancies.

On the second CD-ROM (also known as the Goodies CD), you'll find a bonanza of free stuff! The CD is divided into four sections: stock video, images, After Effects plug-ins, and stock music.

- The Plug-ins folder contains a collection of third-party commercial plug-ins and plug-in demos for After Effects. These plug-ins can add spice to any project.

- The Images folder includes graphics that you can use in your projects without having to pay any royalties. These graphics can be used as simple background plates or layered and animated to create exciting animated sequences.

- The Stock Music folder contains a collection of audio clips. The great thing about these clips is that they can be looped to add as much seamless audio as you need for any project. This time-saving feature can speed up production in any environment.

- The most valuable items on this CD are the stock video clips. You'll find 15 royalty-free video and animation clips from all the major stock libraries, including EyeWire, ArtBeats, Digital Vision, NASA, EyeIdea, and Digital Juice. These clips cover such categories as clouds, water, fire, textures, fabrics, animated backgrounds, and more. Many of these clips come with mattes for easy compositing, or you can simply import them into your video editing application and start using them as backgrounds, special effects, transitions, or plain old stock footage. What's even better is that there's a special offer from the Digital Video Professionals Association (**http://www.dvpa.com**) for even more free stock video!

Resources

Adobe After Effects allows you to make your boss and clients happy while you make a great living. The easiest way to be successful with After Effects is to join a community and network with others who are working in your field. To that end, the following Web sites can help you make the most of your career:

- **http://www.DVPA.com**
- **http://www.RodHarlan.com**
- **http://www.StudioTechniques.com**

Part I

Transfer Modes

The raw artwork supplied for this chapter was created using Adobe Photoshop. Thanks to Scott Kelby, Editor-in-Chief of Photoshop User Magazine, for creating the original collage on which this artwork is based. Images used in the collage come from PhotoDisc.

CHAPTER

1

Creating a Corporate Presentation Opening from a Multi-Layer Photoshop File

Animating Photoshop layers is the basis of many motion graphic elements you find in film, television, DVD, video, and corporate presentations. It's common for motion graphics artists to use layered Photoshop files as a point of departure for designing their animation sequences. I believe that all aspiring motion graphic designers should start their careers learning how to animate Photoshop layers.

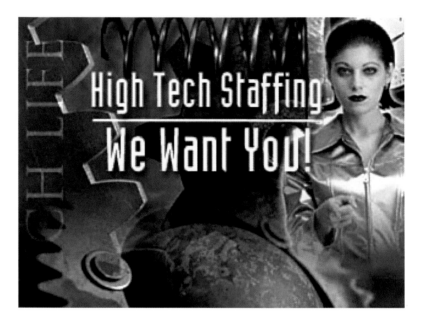

There are millions of graphic designers who make their living working in Adobe Photoshop. It's only natural that Adobe would want to help these designers to become motion graphic artists by making it as easy as possible for them to transfer their skills and artwork to Adobe After Effects. For this reason, Adobe has made integration between After Effects and Photoshop a priority.

For example, there's no need to flatten an image in Photoshop before bringing it into After Effects. After Effects can see, understand, and work with all Photoshop layers. It also sees all of the Photoshop transfer modes and effects applied to a layer. This feature is incredibly powerful because a designer can take a multi-layer file that was designed for print, bring it into After Effects, and animate any layer or effect from the Photoshop file directly in After Effects to produce a final animation.

In this chapter, you'll take a multi-layer Photoshop file, import it into After Effects, and animate the layers to make a quick and exciting corporate presentation.

1. Open a new project by selecting File➡New➡New Project.

2. Import the Photoshop file and all of the graphic layers associated with it by choosing File➡Import➡Photoshop as Comp.

3. Navigate to the Artwork folder for this chapter and select PScollage.psd. Click Open.

4. You now have two items in your Project window: a folder and a composition, both named PScollage.psd. Click on the triangle next to the PScollage.psd folder. Notice that it now displays the contents of the folder.

Now that you've imported the Photoshop file with all six of its layers, it's time to work with them in the After Effects Time Layout window. You'll be adding motion and effects to key layers to bring this project to life. Now would be a good time to save your project.

5. Double-click on the PScollage.psd composition at the bottom of your Project window. This will open the Time Layout window and the Composition window.

6. All of the Photoshop layers have been transferred over to the After Effects Time Layout window in their correct order.

7. Unfortunately, you can't count on After Effects to keep everything correct. Although it keeps the size correct at 320×240, it will set the frame rate and duration to what you used on your last project. To be on the safe side, go to Composition, Composition Settings and set the frame rate to 15 and the duration to 10 seconds. Click OK when done.

8. The last thing you need to do before you begin animating your layers is change each layer's Quality level from Draft to Best. You can do this by clicking once on each of the dotted backslashes to turn them into solid forward slashes.

13

Now you're going to begin working backwards in time. Often, it's easier to set up the final look of the animation first, and then go back to the beginning and make your changes. In this particular case, the Photoshop composition opened with each layer set the way you would like for your animation to end. With a quick keyboard shortcut, you'll be able to lock down these inputs and then go back and animate the start points of each layer:

TIP

In After Effects version 4.1 and beyond, you can click and drag down the layer stack over the eyeball icons, turning on/off video for a series of layers with a single click-and-drag motion.

9. Turn off the visibility of the first four layers by clicking once on each of the eye icons on the left side of the Time Layout window.

10. Hold down the Shift key and select the Gears layer (layer 6) and the Clock layer (layer 5).

11. Move your Time Marker to the 3-second mark in the Time Layout window.

14

12. Type the letter R to open the Rotation parameter control for both of these layers.

13. Now press Option+R on the Mac or Alt+Shift+R on the PC to set a Rotation keyframe at the current value for both of these layers.

14. Type the letter I to go to the In point for both of these layers.

15. Click once on the Rotation value (it probably reads 0.0° because that is what you set the last keyframe value at) on either layer. The changes you make will apply to both layers.

16

16. This opens the Rotation dialog box. Change the degrees to 90. Click OK.

17. Press the spacebar or make a RAM preview to check the rotation of both of these layers.

18. Select the Tech Life layer (layer 3) in the Time Layout window.

19. Turn on the visibility for this layer by clicking once on its eye icon.

20. Move your Time Marker to the 3-second mark in the Time Layout window.

21. Press Option+[on the Mac or Alt+[on the PC to move your layer In point to the 3-second mark.

17

22. Type the letter P to open the Position parameter control for this layer.

23. Click once on the Position stopwatch icon to set a keyframe.

24. Click once on the Position X,Y coordinates.

25. This opens the Position dialog box. Change the Y axis to -235. Make sure that Units is set to pixels. Click OK.

26. Type the letter O to go to the Out point for this layer.

27. Click once on the Position X,Y coordinates (just like you did in step 24).

28. Again, this opens the Position dialog box. This time, change the Y-axis to 250 and click OK.

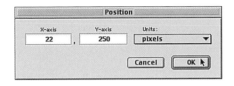

Make another RAM preview. Notice how the text glides over the metallic surface of your background image while allowing a nice see-through effect. This is because the Overlay Transfer mode setting that was applied in Photoshop has been transferred to After Effects.

Now you will animate your two remaining graphic layers. These layers will be used to add extra punch to the final text layer. This would be a good time to save your project.

29. Select the World layer (layer 2).

30. Turn on the visibility for this layer by clicking once on its eye icon.

31. Move your Time Marker to the 5-second mark in the Time Layout window.

32. Type the letter P to open the Position parameter control for this layer.

33. Press Option+P on the Mac or Alt+Shift+P on the PC to set a Position keyframe for this layer.

34. Press Shift+T to open the Opacity parameter control for this layer.

20

35. Now press Option+T on the Mac or Alt+Shift+T on the PC to set an Opacity keyframe for this layer.

36. Move your Time Marker to the 3-second mark in the Time Layout window.

37. Press Option+[on the Mac or Alt+[on the PC to move your layer In point to the 3-second mark.

TIP

You can also use the keyframe navigation arrows or the J key to jump to previous keyframes.

38. Click once on the Position X,Y coordinates.

21

39. This opens the Position dialog box. Change the Y axis to 115. Make sure that Units is set to pixels. Click OK.

40. While still at the 3:00 mark, click once on the Opacity value (100%).

41. This opens the Opacity dialog box. Change the setting from 100% to 0% and click OK to add an Opacity keyframe.

Make another RAM preview. The world graphic now fades in and moves down into position, almost as if the text layer were pushing it into place. But it would probably look better if the world graphic faded in a little bit quicker. No problem. Just move one keyframe. Now would be a good time to save your project.

42. Move your Time Marker to the 4-second mark.

22

43. Select the Opacity keyframe under the 5-second mark in the Time Layout window.

44. Hold down your Shift key and move the Opacity keyframe to the Time Marker located at the 4-second mark.

Presto! A simple one-second dissolve. Now you need to move the girl into place as she sets up your call to action. Her cool, high-tech look, along with pointing finger, will grab the audience's attention.

---

45. Select the Girl layer (layer 4).

TIP

Notice how the keyframe automatically snaps to the Time Marker. If you hold down the Shift key while dragging a keyframe in the Time Layout window, it will automatically snap to the nearest Time Marker or other keyframe, even if those keyframes are on other layers.

Note that if the keyframe is already selected (highlighted), you must click and begin to drag the mouse *before* you press the Shift key. Otherwise, the keyframe will become deselected when you click on it.

23

46. Turn on the visibility for this layer by clicking once on its eye icon.

47. Move your Time Marker to the 7-second mark.

48. Type the letter P to open the Position parameter control for this layer.

49. Now press Option+P on the Mac or Alt+Shift+P on the PC to set a Position keyframe for this layer.

50. Move your Time Marker to the 4-second mark. If you hold down your Shift key, the marker will snap to the keyframe that is already located in that time slot.

51. Press Option+[on the Mac or Alt+[on the PC to move your layer In point to the 4-second mark.

52. Click once on the Position X,Y coordinates.

53. This opens the Position dialog box. Change the Y axis to 530. Make sure that Units is set to pixels. Click OK.

25

Now it's time to bring in the company name, High Tech Staffing, and to tell the audience the purpose of this presentation: "We Want You!" Of course, you can't just dissolve this major point in; you need to use a bit of pizzazz. For this, you will add a quick-streaking blur effect to your slogan. Now would be a good time to save your project.

54. Select the We Want You! layer (layer 1).

55. Turn on the visibility for this layer by clicking once on its eye icon.

56. Go to Layer➡Pre-compose.

57. Select Move all attributes into the new composition and click OK.

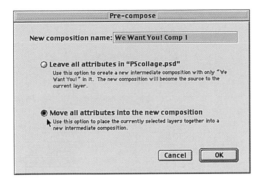

NOTE

Your text layer is smaller than your composition, so unfortunately, any effects that you apply to your text will encounter the boundaries of your layer and look pretty darn ugly (as well as unprofessional). Moving all attributes (that is, the Text layer) into a new composition allows your text to sit on a layer that's the same size as the rest of your composition. Translation: Any effects you add to the text will now go to the edge of your movie, which looks a lot more professional!

58. Move your Time Marker to the 7-second mark.

59. Use the hotkey Option+[on the Mac or Alt+[on the PC to move your layer start point to the 7-second mark.

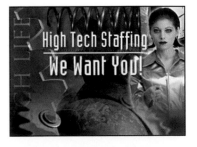

27

60. Go to Effect➡Blur & Sharpen➡Radial Blur.

61. In the Effect Control window that pops up, change Type from Spin to Zoom.

62. Now change Antialiasing from Low to High.

28

Unfortunately, the Radial Blur plug-in is one of the few After Effects plug-ins that does not allow you to set exact amounts or keyframes in the Effect Controls window. You'll need to finish the rest of the settings in the Time Layout window.

63. Type the letter E to reveal the effects applied to the selected layer (in this case Radial Blur) in the Time Layout window.

64. Click once on the Radial Blur triangle to expose the settings.

65. Click once on the Amount value.

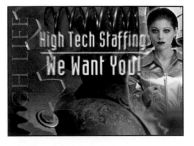

66. This opens the Slider Control dialog box. Change the Value to 700. Click OK.

67. Click once on the Amount stopwatch icon to set a keyframe.

68. Move your Time Marker to the 8-second mark.

69. Click once on the Amount value. This time, set Value to 0 in the Slider Control dialog box and click OK.

Make another RAM preview. Notice how your text now appears to be created from particles in the air. Also, notice how much longer it takes to render a RAM preview. Adding an effect like Radial Blur increases rendering time dramatically because After Effects must calculate the movement of each individual particle across the total amount of frames to which we have applied our effect.

If you're happy with your project after looking at the RAM preview, it's time to render your final movie with all the correct settings for your appropriate output and/or distribution method. Now would be a good time to save your project.

70. With the current Composition or Time Layout window as the active window, or with the composition's name/icon selected in the Project window, go to your menu bar and select Composition➡Make Movie.

31

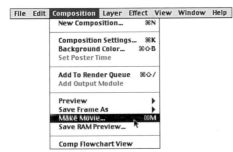

71. A Save Movie As dialog box opens. Save the movie to your desired folder or directory as "We Want You!"

72. The Render Queue opens next. Here you need to change the render settings from Current Settings to Best Settings.

73. Next, click on the underlined Output Module setting and change the Output Module to your choice of format (QuickTime Movie was used in this example). Check Import into project when done so that you can quickly see your movie once it's finished rendering.

74. In the same Output Module Settings dialog box, click on the Format Options button in the Video Output section.

75. The Compression Settings dialog box pops up. For this example, choose Sorenson as your compressor and set it to Best Quality. Click OK twice to get back to the Render Queue.

33

76. When the Render Queue is finally ready, click Render.

After the render is complete, play your movie to make sure it has come out the way you expected. If all is well, save your final project as Photoshop Collage.

The raw artwork supplied for this chapter was created using Adobe Illustrator.

CHAPTER 2

Creating Cartoon Cel Animation from a Multi-Layer Illustrator File

This technique and style of animation are used in a number of TV cartoons and commercials. If you have a good idea for a cartoon series, this is a very good (and inexpensive) way of producing your own pilot episode.

Working with a multi-layer Adobe Illustrator file is very similar to working with a multi-layer Photoshop file. You can import each layer individually, merge them all together, or import them as a composition. Most people use Illustrator art when they want to scale an object hundreds or even thousands of times its normal size without losing any quality. Others use Illustrator for drawing cartoons, logo design and typesetting titles.

Since there are a number of tutorials on the Web and in books on how to infinitely scale an Illustrator graphic, I've decided to show you something different. In this chapter, you'll take a multi-layer Illustrator file, import it into After Effects, and animate the layers to make a fun cel animation-style cartoon.

1. Open a new project by selecting File➡New➡New Project.

File	Edit	Composition	Layer	Effect	View	Window	Help

New ▶   New Project ⌘⌥N
Open... ⌘O   New Folder ⌘⇧⌥N

Close ⌘W
Save ⌘S
Save As...
Save a Copy...
Revert

Import ▶
Export ▶

Add Footage to Comp ⌘/
Consolidate All Footage
Remove Unused Footage
Collect Files...
Watch Folder...

Set Proxy ▶
Interpret Footage ▶
Replace Footage ▶
Reload Footage ⌘⌥L

Preferences ▶
Templates ▶

Recent Footage ▶
Recent Projects ▶

Adobe Online...

Quit ⌘Q

2. Import the Illustrator file and all of the graphic layers associated with it by choosing File➡Import➡Illustrator as Comp.

File	Edit	Composition	Layer	Effect	View	Window	Help

New ▶
Open... ⌘O

Close ⌘W
Save ⌘S
Save As...
Save a Copy...
Revert

Import ▶   Footage File... ⌘I
Export ▶   Footage Files... ⌘⌥I
   Footage As...
Add Footage to Comp ⌘/   Project...
Consolidate All Footage
Remove Unused Footage   Premiere As Comp...
Collect Files...   Photoshop As Comp...
Watch Folder...   Illustrator As Comp...
   Placeholder...
Set Proxy ▶
Interpret Footage ▶
Replace Footage ▶
Reload Footage ⌘⌥L

Preferences ▶
Templates ▶

Recent Footage ▶
Recent Projects ▶

Adobe Online...

Quit ⌘Q

3. Navigate to the Artwork folder for this chapter and select farmer.ai. Click Open.

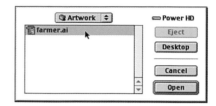

4. You now have two items in your Project window: a folder and a composition, both named farmer.ai. Click on the triangle next to the farmer.ai folder. It now displays the layers within this Illustrator file.

Now that you've imported the Illustrator file, with all eight of its layers, it's time to work with them in the After Effects Time Layout window. You'll be adding motion and effects to specific layers to bring this project to life. Now would be a good time to save your project.

---

5. Double-click on the farmer.ai composition at the bottom of your Project window. This will open the Time Layout window and the Composition window.

TIP

As a general rule, it's a good idea to save your project periodically throughout the creative process. This will save you many headaches in the long run. It's also a good idea to save your project with different names throughout the process (project a, project b, project c, etc.). This way you can go back a few steps if you see that your experimentation has taken you in a different direction than where you want to end up.

6. All of the Illustrator layers now appear as composition layers in the After Effects Time Layout window in their correct order.

7. Unfortunately, you can't count on After Effects to keep everything correct. Although it keeps the size correct at 320×240 (see the following Tip), it sets the frame rate and duration to what you used last. To be on the safe side, go to Composition➡Composition Settings and set the frame rate to 15 and the duration to 15 seconds.

8. The last thing you need to do before you begin animating your layers is change each layer's Quality level from Draft to Best. You can do this by clicking once on each of the dotted backslashes to turn them into solid forward slashes.

TIP

To import Adobe Illustrator files into Adobe After Effects at a specific size, you need to set crop marks in the Illustrator file.

The easiest way to specify a layer's size and set crop marks in Adobe Illustrator is to do the following:

1. Select the Rectangle tool and click once on your document.

2. A dialog box will open. Enter your dimensions (width and height). Click OK.

3. With the rectangle still selected, go to Objects➡Crop Marks➡Make.

If you don't want to be this specific, use the Rectangle tool to draw a rectangle around your Illustrator object. Then set your Stroke and Fill to none so that you don't end up with a black/colored square/outline over your image. Lastly, position your rectangle where you want your cropped edges to be.

37

In Steps 9–13 you're going to fix a problem that sometimes occurs when importing Illustrator files with large areas of color gradiation. Not to worry; After Effects has the fix built into its program. The trick lies in applying the fix to the original file in the Project window and not the layer in the Time Layout window.

9. Look carefully at the layer named Sky (layer 8). It should contain banding (vertical and/or horizontal lines—you may need to magnify). Banding can occur in gradients that are imported from Illustrator into After Effects.

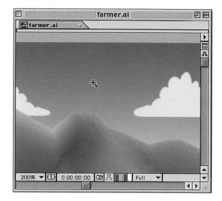

10. To fix the banding problem, select the Sky layer in the Project window.

38

11. Go to File➡Interpret Footage➡Main.

| File | Edit | Composition | Layer | Effect | View | Window | Help |

New ▶
Open... ⌘O

Close ⌘W
Save ⌘S
Save As...
Save a Copy...
Revert

Import ▶
Export ▶

Add Footage to Comp ⌘/
Consolidate All Footage
Remove Unused Footage
Collect Files...
Watch Folder...

Set Proxy ▶
Interpret Footage ▶   Main... ⌘F
Replace Footage ▶   Proxy...
Reload Footage ⌘⌥L
                         Remember Interpretation ⌘⌃C
Preferences ▶   Apply Interpretation ⌘⌃V
Templates ▶

Recent Footage ▶
Recent Projects ▶

Adobe Online...

Quit ⌘Q

12. Click the Options button in the bottom-right corner of the Interpret Footage dialog box.

Interpret Footage

Interpretation for "Sky/farmer.ai"

Alpha
[Guess]   ☐ Inverted
○ Ignore
● Treat As Straight (Unmatted)
○ Treat As Premultiplied (Matted with color)   [ ] 🖊

Frame Rate
○ Use frame rate from file:
○ Assume this frame rate: 30

Fields and Pulldown
Separate Fields: [Off ▼]   ☐ Motion Detect (Best quality only)
Remove Pulldown: [Off ▼]
           [Guess 3:2 Pulldown]

Pixel Aspect Ratio   **Looping**   **Options**
[Square Pixels ▼]   Loop 1 times   [Options...]

                         [Cancel] [OK]

40

13. Change Antialiasing from Faster to More Accurate. Click OK twice to get back to the Project menu.

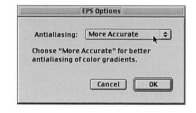

To bring these layers to life, first you must animate the rotation of the wheels. This will simulate the tractor being driven down the road by the farmer. Now would be a good time to save your project.

14. Turn off the visibility of layers 1 and 2 by clicking on their eye icons at the far left of the Time Layout window. This will make it easier for you to work on the tractor and its wheels.

15. Select the back tire (layer 4).

16. Select the Pan Behind tool.

17. Move the anchor point for this layer to the white area in the center of the back tire.

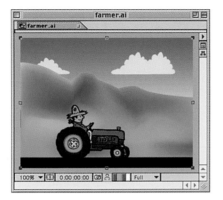

NOTE

Although the After Effects User Guide calls it the Pan Behind tool, you (and everyone else in the world) probably know it as the Anchor Point tool.

It's important to note that the Composition, Time Layout, or Layer window must be the active window for this tool to be active. If the Project window is the active window, the Y key command won't work.

18. Double-check that your Time Marker is still set to 0, and then press the letter R on your keyboard to open the Rotation property.

19. Click once on the tiny Rotation stopwatch icon to set a keyframe. (The Rotation value automatically starts at 0, so you don't need to do anything more.)

41

RAM previews are meant to show portions of the composition rather than the entire thing, and how much you see depends on how much free RAM you have. For this reason, be sure to temporarily adjust your composition's work area markers before creating a RAM preview. The quickest method is to set the Current Time marker at the desired beginning, press the hotkey B, move the marker to the desired end, and press the hotkey N.

With the beginning and end Work Area markers set, there are two methods to create a RAM preview. Go to Window, Show Time Controls (or press Ctrl+3 on the PC or Cmd+3 on the Mac) and click the arrow button on the far right of the Time Controls box. Or, press 0 on your keyboard's numeric keypad.

TIP

If you hold down the Shift key while making a RAM preview, After Effects will only cache *every other frame*. This trick can be a huge timesaver, especially if the only reason you're making a RAM preview is to check the basic motion of your layers.

20. Press the letter O on your keyboard to go to the OUT point of the layer.

21. Click on the underlined 0.0° Rotation value to open the Rotation dialog box.

22. In the Rotation dialog box, change Revolutions to 7. A second Rotation keyframe will be set for you at the current time.

23. Make a RAM preview and look at your rear wheel roll!

42

Now you're going to apply the same rotation to your front wheel. Since the rotation work has already been done, you're going to save yourself some time by copying the settings (keyframes) from your rear wheel to your front wheel.

24. Click once on the word Rotation (note that you're still on the Back Tire layer). Notice how both keyframes become selected.

TIP

To copy, you can also use the keyboard shortcut Ctrl+C on the PC or Cmd+C on the Mac.

25. Go to Edit➡Copy.

43

26. Select the front tire (layer 3).

TIP

Press the letter Y on your keyboard to select the Pan Behind tool.

27. Select the Pan Behind (Anchor Point) tool.

28. Move the anchor point for this layer to the white area in the center of the front tire.

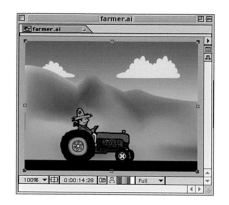

29. Press the letter I on your keyboard to go to the IN point of the layer. Make sure you're at Time Marker 0.00.

30. Press the letter R on your keyboard to open the Rotation property.

31. Go to Edit➡Paste. Your existing keyframes from the rear wheel are now applied to the front wheel.

TIP
To paste, you can also use the keyboard shortcut Ctrl+V on the PC or Cmd+V on the Mac.

File	Edit	Composition	Layer	Effect	View	Window	Help

Undo Copy	⌘Z
Can't Redo	⌘⇧Z
Cut	⌘X
Copy	⌘C
Paste	⌘V
Clear	
Duplicate	⌘D
Split Layer	⌘⇧D
Select All	⌘A
Deselect All	⌘⇧A
Label	▶
Purge	▶
Edit Original...	⌘E

32. Switch back to the Selection tool (/arrow) and turn on the visibility of layers 1 and 2.

NOTE
If your tire layers are wobbling a little too much, you may need to center the anchor point a bit more.

45

farmer.ai
0:00:00:00

			#	Layer Name					
👁		▷ ☐	1	Grass Flowers...					
👁		▷ ☐	2	Road					
👁		▽ ☐	3	Front Tire					
✓ ▶		▷ ⓈRotation		0.0°					
👁		▽ ☐	4	Back Tire					
✓ ▶		▷ ⓈRotation		0.0°					
👁		▷ ☐	5	Tractor					
👁		▷ ☐	6	Hills					
👁		▷ ☐	7	Clouds					

Switches / Modes

Make a RAM preview. Now your tractor looks like it's rolling on down the road. Of course, it would be more realistic if the scenery was moving as well. In steps 33 to 47, you'll animate the Grass&Flowers layer so that it creates a seamless loop of movement. Now would be a good time to save your project.

33. Select the Grass&Flowers layer (layer 1).

farmer.ai
0:00:00:00

			#	Layer Name					
👁		▷ ☐	1	Grass&Flowers					
👁		▷ ☐	2	Road					
👁		▽ ☐	3	Front Tire					
✓ ▶		▷ ⓈRotation		0.0°					
👁		▽ ☐	4	Back Tire					
✓ ▶		▷ ⓈRotation		0.0°					
👁		▷ ☐	5	Tractor					
👁		▷ ☐	6	Hills					
👁		▷ ☐	7	Clouds					

Switches / Modes

34. Press the letter I on your keyboard to go to the IN point of the layer. Make sure the Time Marker is at 0.00.

35. Go to the Effect menu and choose Distort➡Offset.

NOTE

Pressing the letter E on your keyboard reveals any effects that have been applied to your selected layer. In this case, it's the Offset filter.

36. Press the letter E on your keyboard to reveal the Offset effect in the Time Layout window.

37. Click once on the Offset triangle to reveal the Offset control properties.

38. Click once on the Shift Center To stopwatch icon to set a keyframe.

NOTE

The Offset effect pans our image within the layer. Moving your Shift Center To parameter allows for the part of our image that's pushed off one side of the layer to appear on the opposite side. In very simplistic terms, it's like making a loop.

47

39. Click once on the Shift Center To values (they probably read 160.0, 120.0) to open the Shift Center To Point Control dialog box.

40. Change X-axis from 160 to 0.

41. Change Units from Pixels to % of composition. Click OK.

42. Press the letter O on your keyboard to go to the OUT point of the layer.

43. Once again, click on the Shift Center To values (this time they should read 0.0, 120.0) to open the Shift Center To Point Control dialog box.

44. Change X-axis from 0 to -500. Click OK.

45. Now give the layer an extra dash of realism by adding motion blur. Go to the Effect menu and choose Blur & Sharpen➡Motion Blur.

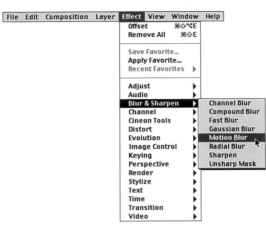

NOTE

It's important to note that you're using the Offset effect to animate the layer, which is not recognized as a geometric transformation. In this case, enabling the Motion Blur switch in the Time Layout window will have no effect on our layer because you're not animating any geometric transformations. For this reason, you must use the Motion Blur filter from the Effect menu.

46. In the Effect Controls window, change the Motion Blur direction to –90°. You can click on the underlined value 0.0 and type in the number, or simply rotate the dial to the left until you reach –90°.

47. Change your Blur Length to 1.0°. Either click on the underlined value 0.0 and type in the number, or simply move the slider to the right until you reach 1.0°.

49

Make a RAM preview. Voilà! Your cheerful farmer is cruising on down the road in his tractor. If this was a longer clip that was part of a larger cartoon storyline, you would want to animate the hills and clouds in the background as well. Just remember that items farther away from the eye are blurry and move slowly.

If you're happy with your project after looking at the RAM preview, it's time to render your final movie with all the correct settings for your appropriate output and/or distribution method. Now would be a good time to save your project.

TIP

You can also use the Make Movie command by pressing Ctrl+M on the PC or Cmd+M on the Mac.

50

48. With the current Composition or Time Layout window as the active window, or with the Composition's name/icon selected in the Project window, go up to your menu bar and select Composition→Make Movie.

File Edit	Composition	Layer Effect View Window Help
	New Composition...	⌘N
	Composition Settings...	⌘K
	Background Color...	⌘⇧B
	Set Poster Time	
	Add To Render Queue	⌘⇧/
	Add Output Module	
	Preview	▶
	Save Frame As	▶
	Make Movie...	⌘M
	Save RAM Preview...	
	Comp Flowchart View	

49. A Save Movie As dialog box opens. Save the movie as Tractor to your desired folder or directory.

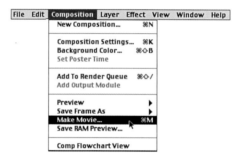

50. The Render Queue opens next. Here you need to change Render Settings from Current Settings to Best Settings.

51. Next, click on the underlined Output Module setting and change the output module to your choice of format (QuickTime Movie was used in this example). Check Import into project when done so that you can quickly see your movie once it's finished rendering.

51

52. In the same Output Module Settings dialog box, click on the Format Options button in the Video Output section.

NOTE

For vector-based graphics, the Animation code is a better choice than Sorenson. The Medium quality setting produces decent results while cutting your file size in half.

53. The Compression Settings dialog box pops up. For this example, choose Animation as your compressor and set the slider to Medium Quality. Click OK twice to get back to the Render Queue.

52

TIP

If you checked the Import into project when done check box in the Output Module, simply double-click on the movie icon in your Project window.

54. When the Render Queue is finally ready, click Render.

TIP

If you plan on sharing your project file with others, especially cross-platform, you need to add the .aep extension to your project name

After the render is complete, play your movie to make sure it came out the way you expected. If all is well, save your final project as Farmer Cartoon.

The raw artwork supplied for this chapter was created using Adobe Illustrator and Adobe Premiere.

CHAPTER 3

Adding Special Effects to a Multi-Layer Premiere File

This technique shows how different types of programs work together to complete a final piece. In this example, a logo is created in an illustration program (Illustrator), video is captured and edited together, and a soundtrack is added in a DV editor (Premiere). Then the whole project is imported into a special effects program (After Effects) to add animation and that extra "Wow!" factor.

After Effects is not a video editing application. You could probably force it to act like one, but you're better off letting After Effects concentrate on what it does best: animation, compositing, and special effects.

A good non-linear video editor will let you play back video clips from the timeline in real-time. After Effects has to render its timeline to RAM or to disk to do this. For this reason, it's a good idea to do all of your basic video editing (trimming clips, placing them in order, adding music) in a program like Adobe Premiere and then import the whole project into Adobe After Effects for the final touches.

In this chapter, you'll import a completed Adobe Premiere project, learn about the problems that occur when importing, and get some ideas on how to jazz up your video piece in Adobe After Effects.

1. Open a new project by selecting File➡New➡New Project.

2. Import the Premiere project and all of the footage files associated with it by choosing File➡Import➡Premiere as Comp.

NOTE

The zTour project and files are the same ones included in the Premiere Demo that's included on the Book CD.

NOTE

If you notice the color bars appearing in the Project window thumbnail after importing zTour.ppj, don't panic. You'll fix this in a few steps.

TIP

You can also import footage by doing the following:

PC—Right-click in the project window, or press Ctrl+I.

Mac—Hold down the Ctrl key and click in the project window, or press Cmd+I.

Or you can simply double-click inside the Project window in the white area (*not* on a file).

3. Navigate to the Artwork folder for this chapter and select zTour.ppj. Click Open.

4. There's still one additional file that you need to add to your project that was not originally part of the Premiere project. To add this graphics file, choose File➡Import➡Footage File.

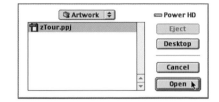

5. Now select VelomanPlain.eps in the Artwork folder for the chapter. Click Open.

6. Your project window should now look like the following figure.

7. Click on the triangle next to the zTour.ppj folder to display its contents.

8. Select Boys.mov by clicking once on the file in the zTour.ppj folder. Notice the color bars at the top and the word "Placeholder" to the side.

If the filename is in italics, the word "Placeholder" is next to it (under the Type heading), and color bars appear in the thumbnail, your files need to be relinked to their original media. This process of relinking media is very simple, and every After Effects user should know how to do it.

9. To relink the footage, double-click on the Boys.mov file in the zTour.ppj folder in your project window. A dialog box opens.

10. Select the Boys.mov file in the Artwork folder for the chapter and click Open.

11. Notice how the word QuickTime now appears under the Type heading, where the word Placeholder used to be. This now shows the correct file type for Boys.mov.

12. Select Cyclers.mov and notice the generic color bars thumbnail icon at the top of the project window. This is another indication that the clip in the AE project window needs to be relinked with its original footage.

NOTE

Most of the time your Premiere project file will import perfectly, with no relinking of media necessary. Creating your basic video piece in a non-linear editor like Premiere can be a huge timesaver. However, the zTour.ppj file forces you to relink media so that you'll know what to do if this situation ever arises. Normally, you'll be able to skip steps 9–16.

13. Double-click on the Cyclers.mov file in the zTour.ppj folder in your project window. A dialog box opens.

14. Once again, select the Cyclers.mov file in the Artwork folder for the chapter and click Open.

59

15. The correct thumbnail icon now appears at the top of the project window. The information to the right of the thumbnail icon now includes the number of colors and compression type used.

60

16. Repeat steps 13 and 14 for the rest of the files in the zTour.ppj folder until all files are relinked with their original media.

Now that you've imported the Premiere project file, all media files, and the additional graphic file that you plan to use for this project, it's time to see what the Premiere project looks like in the After Effects Time Layout window. You'll also learn about the parts of a Premiere project that After Effects does not import and how you can fix this. Now would be a good time to save your project.

17. Double-click on the zTour.ppj composition at the bottom of your Project window. This will open the Time Layout window and the Composition window.

18. All of the Premiere timeline has been transferred over to After Effects, including video, audio, and graphic files. The faintly colored outline (white area) before or after each individual layer shows you where the original clip was trimmed in Premiere.

19. However, not all items transfer seamlessly from Premiere to After Effects. Layer 6 is a cross dissolve that was not imported. Select this layer by clicking on it once with your mouse.

20. Now press the Delete key on your keyboard to send this layer into oblivion.

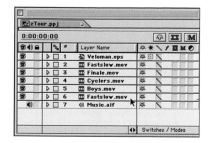

At this point, there are a number of ways to add a dissolve-type effect to the required clips. This will replace the cross dissolve that did not transfer over from Premiere. The following steps show just one possibility.

21. Select the Fastslow.mov file, which is now layer 6.

22. Move the Fastslow.mov file from layer 6 to in-between Finale.mov and Cyclers.mov (layers 3 and 4).

62

23. With Fastslow.mov still selected, press the letter I on your keyboard to go to the IN point of the layer.

24. Now press the letter T on your keyboard to reveal the Opacity property.

25. Click once on the Opacity stopwatch icon to set an Opacity keyframe.

TIP

Wherever you see an underlined value in After Effects, you can click on it to enter the value numerically in a dialog box.

26. Next, click on the underlined 100% Opacity value to open up the Opacity dialog box.

RAM previews are meant to show portions of the composition rather than the entire thing, and how much you see depends on how much free RAM you have. For this reason, be sure to temporarily adjust your composition's work area markers before creating a RAM preview. The quickest method is to set the Current Time marker at the desired beginning, press the hotkey B, move the marker to the desired end, and press the hotkey N.

With the beginning and end Work Area markers set, there are two methods to create a RAM preview. Go to Window, Show Time Controls (or press Ctrl+3 on the PC or Cmd+3 on the Mac) and click the arrow button on the far right of the Time Controls box. Or, press 0 on your keyboard's numeric keypad.

64

If you hold down the Shift key while making a RAM preview, After Effects will only cache *every other frame*. This trick can be a huge timesaver, especially if the only reason you're making a RAM preview is to check the basic motion of your layers.

27. In the Opacity settings window, change the setting to 0%. Click OK.

28. Move the Time Marker to 8:00 seconds.

29. Click on the 0% Opacity value to open up the Opacity settings window again, but this time, type in a setting of 100%. Click OK.

30. Make a RAM preview and check out your new dissolve transition.

Now it's time to give your logo a little love. Right now, the Veloman.eps logo... well... it just sits there. No life, no action, just a big fat logo sitting on top of your video. The next few steps will bring your logo to life. Now would be a good time to save your project.

31. Select the Veloman.eps file in the Time Layout window (layer 1).

32. Click once on the Quality switch to set it to Best (you should see a forward slash).

33. Press the letter I on your keyboard to go to the IN point of the layer.

34. Press the letter S on your keyboard to reveal the Scale property for this layer.

NOTE

Continuous rasterization means recalculating a file's resolution inside of the project whenever you preview or render so it displays at full resolution regardless of size.

35. Click once on the Scale stopwatch icon to set a Scale keyframe.

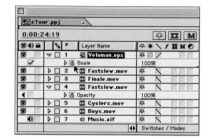

NOTE

There's no need to turn on Continuous Rasterization because the graphics Scale will be at 100% or less. Just make sure your quality setting is set to Best when you render.

36. Next, click on the 100% Scale value to open up the Scale settings dialog box.

66

TIP

Restricting your vector graphics Scale parameter to 100% or less allows After Effects to treat it like any other pixel-based graphic, and it will automatically anti-alias your object. Not enabling Continuous Rasterization when your Scale is set at 100% or less will save you render time.

37. In the Scale settings dialog box, change the setting to 0% of the source. Make sure that Preserve Frame Aspect Ratio is selected. Click OK.

38. Move the Time Marker to 27:00 seconds.

39. Click on the 0% Scale value to open up the Scale settings dialog box. This time, type in a setting of 100% to add a second Scale keyframe. Click OK.

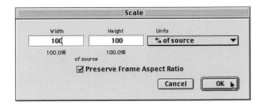

If you make a RAM preview or press the Spacebar on your keyboard to play through the work you've just completed, you'll will see that you've scaled the logo from nothing to full-screen over the background clip of your cyclists. This is okay, but a little more animation will make it better. Now would be a good time to save.

40. With the Veloman.eps file still selected, press the letter I on your keyboard to go to the IN point of the layer.

41. Press the letter R on your keyboard to open up the Rotation property.

42. Click once on the Rotation stopwatch icon to set a keyframe. (Since the Rotation control automatically starts at 0, you don't need to do anything more.)

43. Press the letter O on your keyboard to go to the OUT point of the layer.

44. Click on the underlined 0.0° Rotation value to open up the Rotation settings dialog box.

45. In the Rotation settings dialog box, change Revolutions to 3. Click OK.

Make a RAM preview to see your animated logo, which scales up to full size while rotating. Not bad. But all this was to make up for the properties that weren't imported from Premiere. Now it's time to add some compositing tricks that are unique to After Effects. You will now create a "window to the world" effect, with all of your footage taking place inside of the basic shape of your Veloman logo. Now would be a good time to save your project.

46. Create a new composition by choosing Composition➡New Composition.

TIP

You can also create a new composition by pressing Ctrl+N on the PC or Cmd+N on the Mac.

47. In the Composition Settings dialog box, place your Premiere project in a 320×240 composition window because this will be the size of your finished movie. You're going to work at 15 frames per second, with a duration of 30 seconds. Name the composition Veloman Final. Click OK when you're done.

69

48. Drag the zTour.ppj composition from the Project window to the Time Layout window.

49. Make sure the Time Marker is still set at 0:00, and drag the VelomanPlain.eps file from the Project window to the Time Layout window.

70

50. Change the background color of your composition by choosing Composition➡Background Color.

51. Click once on the eyedropper icon in the Background Color dialog box.

52. Now click on the beige VelomanPlain.eps graphic in the Composition window. Click OK.

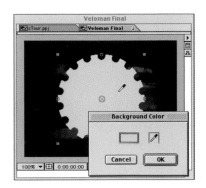

NOTE
You're clicking on the beige VelomanPlain.eps graphic to sample this color as your background color.

71

53. Click once on the Quality switch to set VelomanPlain.eps (layer 1) to Best (you should see a forward slash).

Notice how the background color of your composition is now the exact color of your logo. Here's where the magic begins.

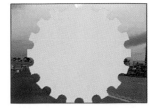

54. In the Time Layout window, select zTour.ppj (layer 2).

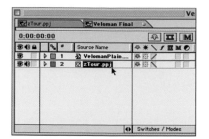

55. Change your view to Modes by clicking once on Switches/Modes at the bottom of the Time Layout window.

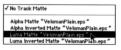

56. Change the track matte for zTour.ppj (layer 2) from None to Luma Matte "VelomanPlain.eps".

<table>
<tr><td>√ No Track Matte</td></tr>
<tr><td>Alpha Matte "VelomanPlain.eps"
Alpha Inverted Matte "VelomanPlain.eps"
Luma Matte "VelomanPlain.eps"
Luma Inverted Matte "VelomanPlain.eps"</td></tr>
</table>

Make a RAM preview or press the Spacebar on your keyboard to play through the work you've just completed. You've created a "window to the world" effect, with all of your footage taking place inside of the basic shape of your Veloman logo. Now let's add a little movement to this window. Now would be a good time to save.

NOTE

Track Matte sets up a matte and fill relationship between two layers positioned on top of each other in the layer stack. Once enabled, the Track Matte allows the bottom layer to show through areas of the top layer based on the top layer's alpha or luminance values.

A Luma Matte allows the bottom layer to show through areas of the top layer that have luminance values of greater than 0%. Areas that have luminance values of 100% are completely opaque, and those with values between 1% and 99% are semitransparent.

57. Change your view back to Switches by clicking once on Switches/Modes at the bottom of the Time Layout window.

58. Select VelomanPlain.eps (layer 1) and press the letter I on your keyboard to bring you back to Time Marker 0:00.

59. Press the letter R on your keyboard to bring up the Rotation property.

60. Click once on the Rotation stopwatch icon to set a keyframe. (Since the Rotation control automatically starts at 0, you don't need to do anything more.)

61. Press the letter O on your keyboard to go to the OUT point of the layer.

62. Click on the underlined 0.0° Rotation value to open up the Rotation settings dialog box.

63. In the Rotation settings dialog box, change Revolutions to –2. Click OK.

74

Now make a RAM preview or scrub through the Time Layout window using the jog shuttle. Notice the counterclockwise rotation of your "window to the world." This effect works especially well in the last five seconds of the composition, contrasted against the clockwise rotation of the Veloman logo. If it looks the way you want it to, move on to the next steps. If not, go back and change the number of revolutions.

NOTE
You change the number of revolutions to adjust the speed. The more revolutions, the faster it spins. The fewer revolutions, the slower the rotation.

If you're happy with your project after looking at the RAM preview, it's time to render your final movie with all the correct settings for your appropriate output and/or distribution method. Now would be a good time to save your project. See the adjacent note about increasing and decreasing revolutions.

64. With the current Composition or Time Layout window as the active window, or with the composition's name/icon selected in the Project window, go up to your menu bar and select Composition➡Make Movie.

TIP
You can also do the Make Movie command by pressing Ctrl+M on the PC or Cmd+M on the Mac.

75

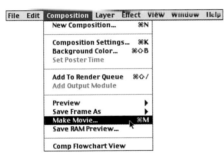

65. A Save Movie As dialog box opens. Save the movie as Veloman.mov to your desired folder or directory.

66. The Render Queue opens next. Here you need to change Render Settings from Current Settings to Best Settings.

67. Next, click on the underlined Output Module setting and change the output module to your choice of format (QuickTime Movie was used in this example). Check Import into project when done so you can quickly see your movie once it's finished rendering.

68. In the same Output Module Settings dialog box, click on the Format Options button in the Video Output section.

69. The Compression Settings dialog box pops up. Choose Sorenson Video as your compressor, and set it to Best quality. Click OK.

Compression Settings

Compressor
| Sorenson Video ▼ |
| Color |

Quality
Least — Low — Medium — High — Best

Motion
Frames per second: 15 ▼
☐ Key frame every [ ] frames
☐ Limit data rate to [ ] K/Second

Options... | Cancel | OK

70. Since this project has an audio track, click on the Audio Output check box and use these settings: 22.050 KHz, 8 Bit, Mono. Click OK.

☑ Audio Output
Format Options...
| 22.050 KHz ▼ | 8 Bit ▼ | Mono ▼ |
Cancel | OK

NOTE

If the Audio Output check box is not checked, no audio will be rendered.

77

TIP

If you checked the Import into project when done checkbox in the Output Module, simply double-click on the movie icon in your Project window.

71. When the render queue is finally ready, click Render.

Project Untitled.aep • Render Queue

All Renders
Message:
RAM:
Renders Started: Render
Total Time Elapsed:

Log File:

Current Render
                    Elapsed: Est. Remain:

▷ Current Render Details
Render			Comp Name	Status	Started	Render Time
☑	☐	1	Veloman Final	Queued	"	"
▷ Render Settings: ▼ Best Settings		Log: Errors Only ▼
▷ Output Module: ▼ Based on "Lossless"		Output To: Veloman.mov

TIP

If you plan on sharing your project file with others, especially cross-platform, you need to add the .aep extension to your project name.

After the render is complete, play your movie to make sure it came out the way you expected. If all is well, save your final project as Veloman Premiere.

Part II

Text and Number Effects

The raw artwork supplied for this chapter was created using Kinetix 3D Studio MAX. You'll need the Production Bundle version of After Effects to complete this tutorial.

CHAPTER

4

Creating Floating Text on Water

Although this chapter uses basic text to show off this technique's simplicity, a graphic or company logo could be substituted to create a nice corporate image package. This technique has also been used in numerous commercials.

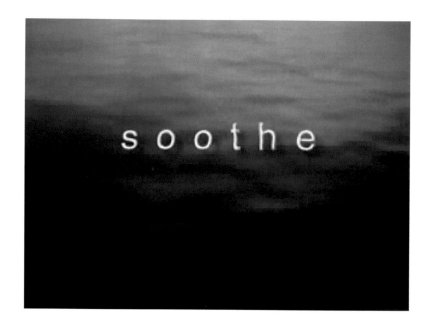

A sports therapy client wants an animation that has legible text but that also conveys a clear sense of the soothing therapy they offer. The budget for the project is such that there's not enough time for lots of hand-animating. A large part of the client's operation deals with various water therapies, so it seems natural to use water in their project. Thanks to After Effect's displacement capabilities, this project can be completed with only one piece of artwork and absolutely no keyframes or hand animation. Plus, it's nice to watch after a long day in front of your monitor.

1. Open a new project by clicking File➡New➡New Project.

2. Create a new composition by choosing Composition➡New Composition.

TIP

You can also create a new composition by pressing Ctrl+N on the PC or Cmd+N on the Mac.

3. In the Composition Settings dialog box, animate your text in a 320×240 composition window because this will be the size of your finished movie. You're going to work at 15 frames per second, with a duration of six seconds. Name the composition Wave text. Click OK when you're done.

TIP

You can also import footage by doing the following:

PC—Right-click in the project window, or press Ctrl+I.
Mac—Hold down the Ctrl key and click in the project window, or press Cmd+I.

Or you can simply double-click inside the Project window in the white area (*not* on a file).

4. To add the video you will be using, choose File➡Import➡Footage File.

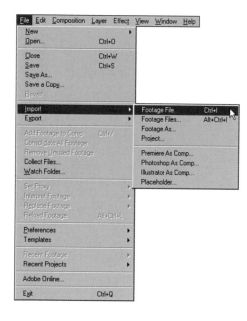

5. Now select water.mov in the Artwork folder for the chapter.

Now that you've imported the movie file that you plan to use for this project, it's time to move it from the Project window to the Time Layout window. You'll also add some text and effects to this project. Now would be a good time to save your project.

6. Drag the water.mov file from the Project window into the Time Layout window.

7. Create a new layer by going to Layer➞New Solid.

83

8. Make sure this layer is set at 320×240 and name it Text. For now, the color doesn't matter, so click OK.

9. Go to Effect menu and choose Text➡Basic Text.

10. The Basic Text dialog box opens. Select a font and type the word "soothe". Make sure that Direction is set to Horizontal and Alignment is set to Center, and then click OK.

11. The Effect Controls window opens up to reveal the different parameters that can be set. Change the Fill color to white and duplicate the settings in the following screen shot to adjust tracking and size.

12. In the Composition window, click on the Action Safe/Title Safe button to check the text's placement. You want the text to be slightly above center for this project.

TIP

There is a way to check the adjustments of any of the variables with sliders as you move them. Just click on the slider and Alt+drag on the PC or Option+drag on the Mac to get a dynamic preview in the main comp window.

85

NOTE

For steps 13–17, make sure that your Text layer is still selected in the Time Layout window. You'll be applying the following effects to the Text layer.

In steps 13–19 you will start to give your text a little life. You will begin by giving your letters an edge (using Bevel Alpha), animating their movement on the water (using Displacement Map), and adding some depth and dimension (using Drop Shadow).

13. Now go to Effect➡Perspective➡Bevel Alpha.

14. In the Effect Controls window, accept the default settings for the Bevel Alpha effect as shown in the following screenshot.

15. Go to the Effect menu and choose Distort➡Displacement Map.

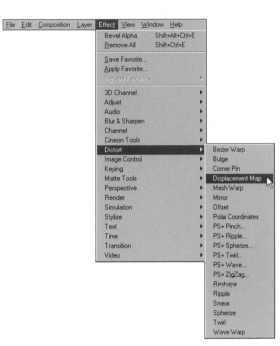

16. In the Effect Controls window for the Displacement Map effect, duplicate the settings shown in the following screenshot.

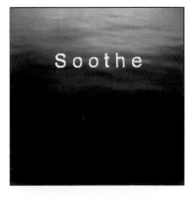

17. Be sure to pay special attention and change the Displacement Map layer parameter to water.mov.

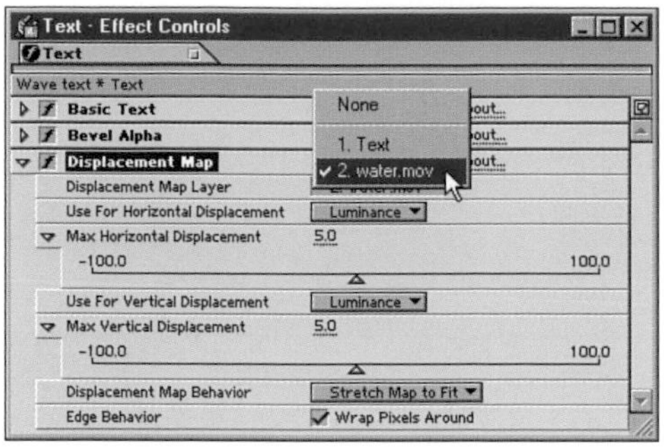

NOTE

RAM previews are meant to show portions of the composition rather than the entire thing, and how much you'll see depends on how much free RAM you have. For this reason, be sure to temporarily adjust your composition's Work Area Markers before creating a RAM preview. The quickest method is to set the Current Time marker to the desired beginning frame, and press the hotkey B, move the marker to the desired ending frame, and press the hotkey N.

With the beginning and end Work Area markers set for the Work Area, there are two methods for creating a RAM preview. You can go to Window, Show Time Controls (or press Ctrl+3 on the PC or Cmd+3 on the Mac) and click the arrow button on the far-right side of the Time Controls box. Or, simply press 0 on your keyboard's numeric keypad.

18. Now go to the Effect menu and choose Perspective➡Drop Shadow.

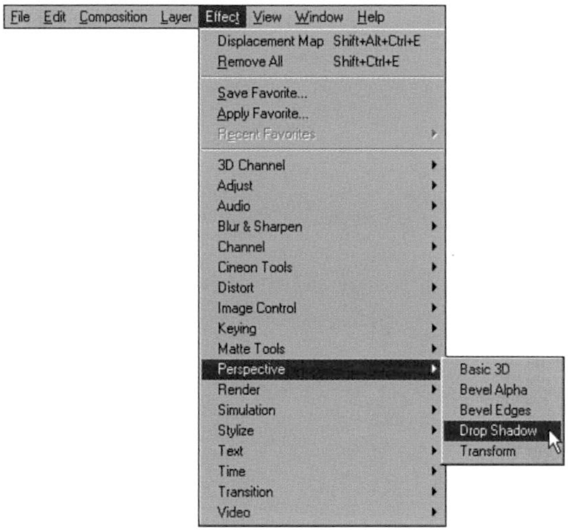

19. In the Effect Controls window for the Drop Shadow effect, duplicate the settings shown in the following screenshot.

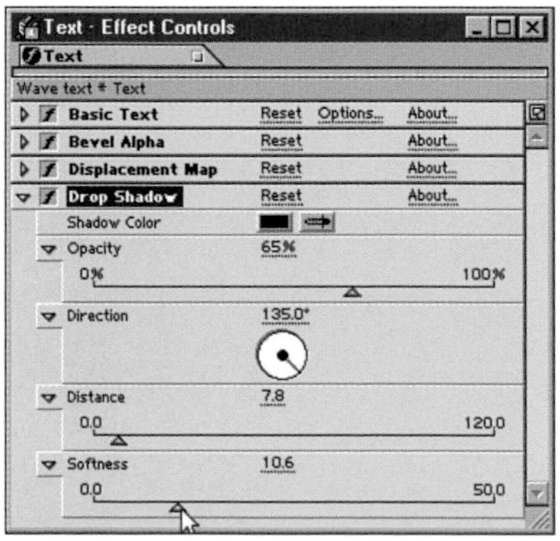

Now make a RAM preview and check the motion of your text. If it looks the way you want it to, move on to the next steps. If not, go back and tweak some of your parameter settings in the Effect Controls window.

If you're happy with your project after looking at the RAM preview, it's time to render your final movie with all the correct settings for your appropriate output and/or distribution method. Now would be a good time to save your project.

20. With the current Composition or Time Layout window as the active window, or with the composition's name/icon selected in the Project window, go up to your menu bar and select Composition➡Make Movie.

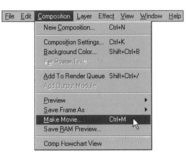

89

21. A Save Movie As dialog box opens. Save the movie as Soothe to your desired folder or directory.

22. The Render Queue opens next. Here you need to change the render settings from Current Settings to Best Settings.

23. Next, click on the underlined Output Module setting and change the output module to your choice of format (QuickTime Movie was used in this example). Check Import into project when done so you can quickly see your movie once it's finished rendering.

24. In the same Output Module Settings dialog box, click on the Format Options button in the Video Output section.

25. The Compression Settings dialog box pops up. For this example, choose Sorenson Video as your compressor and set it to Best quality. Click OK.

26. When the render queue is finally ready, click Render.

TIP

If you checked the Import into project when done check box in the Output Module, simply double-click on the movie icon in your Project window.

TIP

If you plan on sharing your project file with others, especially cross-platform, you need to add the .aep extension to your project name.

After the render is complete, play your movie to make sure it came out the way you expected. If all is well, save your final project as Wavy Text.

The raw artwork supplied for this chapter was created using Adobe Photoshop and Discreet 3D Studio Max.

CHAPTER
5

Making Text Follow a Complicated Path

This type of effect is a staple in broadcast work. However, it's usually done in a robust 3D program. The advantage of doing this in After Effects is that the project will render much faster. This type of effect is used everywhere, from commercials to corporate video, logo IDs to fundraisers.

Creating the effect of animated text following a path is one of the most common tasks for a motion graphic designer. Often it's a very easy project due to the simplicity of the motion that the client requires. For a more demanding path shape, it can require quite a bit of tweaking to get the correct results. Either way, once you learn the basics of how this effect is accomplished, you can go on and add as much complexity as you please without ever having to leave the After Effects interface.

1. Open a new project by clicking File➡New➡New Project.

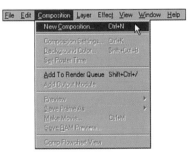

2. Create a new composition by choosing Composition➡New Composition.

3. In the Composition Settings dialog box, animate your text in a 320×240 composition window because this will be the size of your finished movie. You're going to work at 15 frames per second, with a duration of five seconds. Name the composition Stairs and click OK when you're done.

4. To add the graphic that you'll be working with, choose File➡Import➡Footage File.

5. Select staircase.psd in the Artwork folder for the chapter.

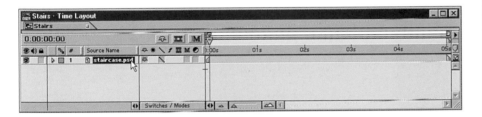

Now that you've imported the artwork file that you plan to use for this project, it's time to move it from the Project window to the Time Layout window. You'll do this, as well as create a mask (a basic outline) of the stairs, in steps 6–12. Now would be a good time to save your project.

---

6. Place the staircase image in the Time Layout window.

7. Double-click on this layer to access its Layer window.

TIP

You can also import footage by doing the following:

PC—Right-click in the project window, or press Ctrl+I.
Mac—Hold down the Ctrl key and click in the project window, or press Cmd+I.

Or you can simply double-click inside the Project window in the white area (*not* on a file).

TIP

As a general rule, it's always a good idea to save your project period-ically throughout the creative process. This will save you many headaches in the long run. It's also a good idea to save your project with different names through-out the process (project a, project b, project c, etc.). This way you can go back a few steps if you see that your experi-mentation has taken you in a different direction than where you want to end up.

NOTE

A Layer window is used to view a composition's layers, to trim footage, and to work with masks.

NOTE

Here you're going to create a path that your letters can follow.

8. It may be a good idea to resize the window to give you more room to create your path.

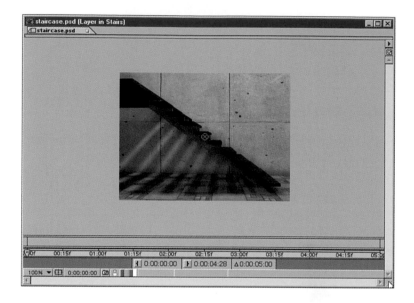

TIP

Pressing the G hotkey also selects the Pen tool.

9. Select the Pen tool.

10. In the new window (your Layer window), carefully outline the stairs. You may find it easier to start from the bottom and work your way to the top.

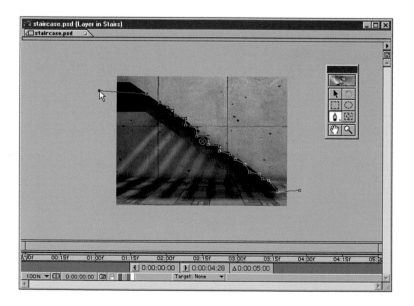

11. Once the basic outline is done, toggle through the Pen tools and select the Add points tool.

12. Using the Add points tool and the Selection (arrow) tool, refine the path by adding or adjusting corners for the front and back edges of the steps. The path should be flat at the top of each step and slightly angled between steps (so it appears the text is falling with momentum). Adjust your path until it closely resembles the following figure and then close this window.

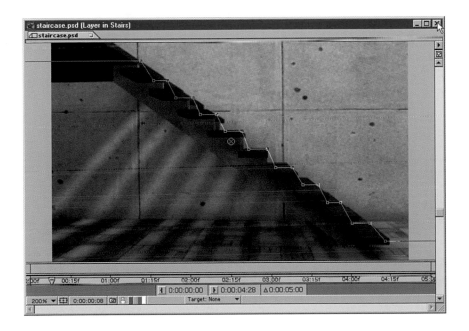

In steps 13–29, you'll add the text and animate it to roll down the stairs like marbles. Now would be a good time to save your project.

97

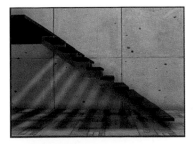

TIP

You can also create a new solid by pressing Ctrl+Y on the PC or Cmd+Y on the Mac.

13. Create a new blank layer for your text by going to Layer➡New Solid.

14. Name this new solid Text, make sure its size is set to 320×240, and click OK.

15. Go to Effect, Text, Path Text.

16. Type in the text you'll be using. For this example, try "WOOO!" Click OK when you're finished.

99

NOTE

I chose the Arial font because I figured most people would have it installed on their systems and it would be the easiest to follow along with in this tutorial. However, unless you want to be laughed at by all the font snobs that now inhabit your planet, please choose a more appropriate font from your own personal collection before showing this technique to a client.

17. Select the staircase.psd layer and click the triangle to the left of the layer name to reveal the Mask Shape property.

18. Highlight Mask 1 by clicking on it once.

TIP

Pressing the M hotkey opens the Mask Shape property.

19. Go to the Edit menu and choose Copy.

TIP

Press Ctrl+C on the PC or Cmd+C on the Mac to copy the mask, and press Ctrl+V on the PC or Cmd+V on the Mac to paste the mask into another layer.

20. Select the text layer.

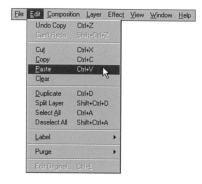

21. Go to the Edit menu and choose Paste. You have now copied the mask from one layer to another.

NOTE

When you double-click the text layer, you're opening its Layer window to view the mask on that layer. The masking tools can be used to create paths in addition to mask shapes.

22. Double-click the text layer to verify that the mask is in place. Close the Layer window when you're done.

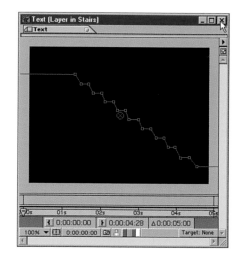

23. Go to the Effect Controls window for the Path Text effect and change Path from None to Mask 1.

24. Also, if you started drawing your path from the bottom of the stairs, be sure to check the Reverse Path box.

25. At this point, you may want to resize and/or adjust the tracking of your text by changing some of the settings in the Effect Controls window. For this example, the tracking is set to 9 and the size is set to 18.

26. Now you need to animate the left margin to make your text move along the path. While on the first frame, click on the Left Margin slider and Alt+drag on the PC or Option+drag on the Mac until the text is at a good starting point in the main comp window.

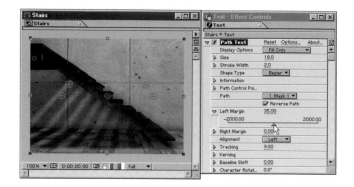

27. Alt+click (or Option+click, on the Mac) on Left Margin to set a keyframe.

28. Move your Time Marker to the end of the comp, and then Alt+drag on the PC or Option+drag on the Mac directly on the Left Margin slider to move the text off the screen (at the bottom-right corner). Notice how a second keyframe is set automatically.

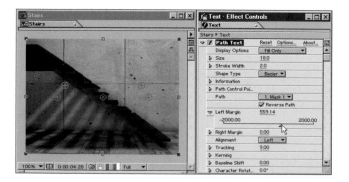

29. Make a RAM preview.

At this point, you may want to repeat steps 6 and 13 to further refine your path. If not, it's time to add a couple of effects to strengthen the look of your text animation. Now would be a good time to save your project.

---

30. With the Text Layer selected, go to Effect➡Perspective➡Bevel Alpha.

31. Accept the default settings.

32. Go to Effect➡Blur & Sharpen➡Motion Blur.

33. Set Direction to -68.0 and Blur Length to 1.

Take a moment to notice how your text is moving quite energetically in the downward direction of the staircase. The only problem is that the text seems to be floating beside the stairs, not actually on them. To remedy this, you'll modify and then close your original path. Specifically, in steps 34 and 35 you will use the Pen and Selection tools to complete these modifications and make it appear as though the letters are actually rolling down the stairs.

34. Switching between the Pen and Add Control Point tools, reshape the top step and then pull out the ends of the path on the staircase.psd layer until your path closely resembles the following figure.

> **NOTE**
>
> The Pen tool automatically switches to the other tools when placed over different points/portions of your path. You can hold down the Ctrl key on the PC or the Cmd key on the Mac to switch between the Pen tool and the selection tools when adjusting a path or mask shape.

> **NOTE**
>
> At this point, you need to closely outline the top step's shape so the text appears behind it.

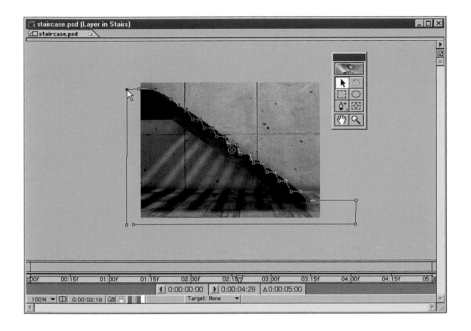

35. With the ends close together, go to Layer➡Mask and select Closed. Close the Layer window when finished.

36. Move the staircase.psd layer to the top of the layer stack in Time Layout window.

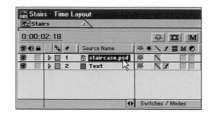

37. From the Project window, pull another copy of staircase.psd onto the Time Layout window and place it at the bottom of the layer stack. Make sure you're still at time marker 0:00.

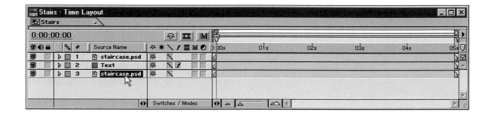

38. You may find it helpful to temporarily disable the Motion Blur effect to see how the text is interacting with the stairs. If so, toggle the f box off in the Effects Control window.

39. Toggle Motion Blur back on.

Save your project, make another RAM preview and adjust the closed mask if necessary. You may need to adjust your mask on both the text layer and the top staircase.psd layer.

If you're happy with your project after looking at the RAM preview, it's time to render your final movie with all the correct settings for your appropriate output and/or distribution method. Now would be a good time to save your project.

40. With the current Composition or Time Layout window as the active window, or with the composition's name/icon selected in the Project window, go up to your menu bar and select Composition➡Make Movie.

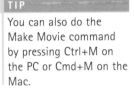

TIP

You can also do the Make Movie command by pressing Ctrl+M on the PC or Cmd+M on the Mac.

107

41. A Save Movie As dialog box opens. Save the movie to your desired folder or directory as Stairs.avi.

42. The Render Queue opens next. Here you need to change Render Settings from Current Settings to Best Settings.

43. Next, click on the underlined Output Module setting and change the output module to your choice of format (QuickTime Movie was used in this example). Check Import into project when done so you can quickly see your movie once it's finished rendering.

44. In the same Output Module Settings dialog box, click on the Format Options button in the Video Output section.

45. The Compression Settings dialog box. For this example, choose Sorenson Video as your compressor and set it to Best quality. Click OK when you're done.

TIP

If you checked the Import into project when done check box in the Output Module, simply double-click on the movie icon in your Project window.

TIP

If you plan on sharing your project file with others, especially cross-platform, you need to add the .aep extension to your project name.

46. When the Render Queue is finally ready, click Render.

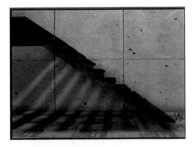

After the render is complete, play your movie to make sure it came out the way you expected. If all is well, save your final project as Text on Path.

The raw artwork supplied for this chapter was created using Discreet 3D Studio Max.

CHAPTER

6

Creating an Animated Signature

This type of effect is a staple in broadcast work, but many times it's completed in a robust 3D program. The advantage of doing this in After Effects is that the project will render much faster. This type of effect is used everywhere, from commercials to corporate video, logo IDs to fundraisers.

So your client wants a word to write itself out on top of an image. One method that you may have seen in the past reveals the text by animating a hand-drawn mask. The method is difficult and prone to error, and worst of all, it only reveals one letter! This project shows a much simpler, more intuitive method that allows you to reveal a letter, a word, or even an entire phrase quickly and easily. What once seemed too difficult to undertake will now become part of your standard effects set that you offer to future clients.

1. Open a new project by clicking File➡New➡New Project.

2. Create a new composition by going to the Composition menu and choosing New Composition.

3. In the Composition Settings dialog box, animate your logo in a 320×240 composition window because this will be the size of your finished movie. You're going to work at 15 frames per second, and with a duration of 3 seconds and 12 frames. Name the composition Write-on and click OK when you're done.

4. To add the video footage that you will be using, select File→Import→Footage File.

5. Select collector.mov in the Artwork folder for the chapter.

You'll create the rest of the information and graphics you need for this project directly in After Effects. In steps 6–12, you'll create the text that you'll use for the write-on effect. Now would be a good time to save your project.

6. Create a new solid by choosing Layer➡New Solid. Name it Text.

113

7. Check that the remaining default settings match these settings.

8. Turn on the Action Safe & Title Safe Guides.

9. While the text layer is selected, go to Effect➡Text➡Basic Text.

10. Type in "Classified" in the font of your choice and click OK.

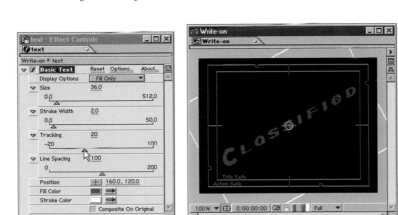

11. Select the Rotate tool and rotate the layer so that it's diagonal.

TIP
Press the hotkey W to select the Rotate tool.

115

12. In the Effect Controls window, adjust the Basic Text tracking so that "Classified" just barely fits in the Title Safe frame.

TIP
There is a way to check the adjustments as you move the slider. Just click on the slider and Alt+drag (or Option+drag on the Mac) to get a dynamic preview in the main comp window.

In steps 13–30, you'll add and animate the effect that writes the text onto the screen. You'll be using the Write-on effect to reveal the text layer, with the help of the Paint Time and Brush Time Properties. Now would be a good time to save your project.

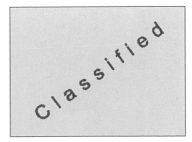

13. With the text layer selected in the Time Layout Window, go to Edit➡Duplicate.

14. Turn off the lower text layer's visibility by clicking on the layer's video switch (the little eye icon) on the left side of the Time Layout window.

15. Select the top text layer and go to Effect➡Stylize➡Write-on.

116

16. A small dot appears on the screen (known as the Brush Position point control). This is the brush head you will be animating.

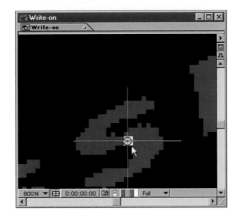

17. Set your Brush Size and Position settings so that they match the following screenshot.

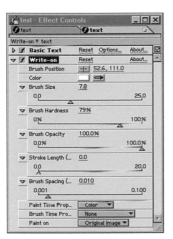

117

NOTE

You may have to come back and tweak the settings slightly, depending on what font you choose. You want your brush size to fit the size of the font pretty closely. As you continue through this project, you'll discover that if the brush is too big, portions of the text appear too soon, especially at the curves.

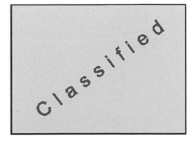

18. Set Paint Time Property to Opacity and Brush Time Property to Size.

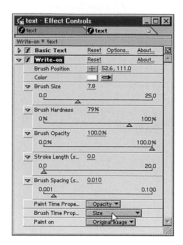

19. Set a keyframe at the first frame by Alt+clicking (or Option+clicking on the Mac) on Brush Position.

20. Now comes the slow part. You'll move ahead one or two frames in the Time Layout window...

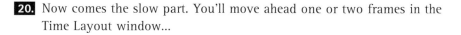

21. ...and move the Brush Position to match. (Keep in mind that you must reveal the text in under three seconds because that's the length of your video.)

22. Each move will set a new keyframe for Brush Position. Continue this process until the entire word has been covered.

23. To get an idea of how this will look when you're finished, view write-on fx.mov in the Artwork folder for this chapter.

119

> **NOTE**
>
> To speed things along, make sure that Write-on is highlighted in the Effect Controls window, and then click on Brush Position and Alt+drag on the PC or Option+drag on the Mac. This will give you instant feedback on how the paint is being laid out.

> **NOTE**
>
> Depending on the font you choose, you may also want to keyframe the brush size so that it's tighter at the thin portions of the letters. Unlike Brush Position, you won't need to set a key every frame or two. Be careful to set a keyframe just before each change of the brush size. Otherwise it will change from the first frame, and this probably isn't what you want.

120

24. Make a RAM preview.

25. If you're pleased with the brush animation, toggle Switches/Modes on the Time Layout window to Modes.

26. Change text layer 2's track matte (the bottom text layer) from No Track Matte to Alpha Matte "text".

27. Turn the visibility back on for text layer 2 by once again clicking the layer's Video Switch (the little eye icon) on the far left of the Time Layout window.

28. In the Effect Controls window, set the Write-On Paint control to Transparent.

29. Now it's time to add the background movie. Drag the collector.mov file from the project window to the Time Layout window.

30. Move collector.mov to the bottom of the layer stack in the Time Layout window.

Make another RAM preview. If you're happy with your project after looking at the RAM preview, it's time to render your final movie with all the correct settings for your appropriate output and/or distribution method. Now would be a good time to save your project.

NOTE

Track Matte sets up a matte-and-fill relationship between two layers positioned on top of each other in the layer stack. Once enabled, the Track Matte allows the bottom layer to show through areas of the top layer based on the top layer's alpha or luminance values.

An Alpha matte allows the bottom layer to show through areas of the top layer that have alpha channel pixel values of greater than 0%. Areas that have alpha channel pixel values of 100% are completely opaque, and those with values between 1% and 99% are semitransparent.

A Luma matte allows the bottom layer to show through areas of the top layer that have luminance values of greater than 0%. Areas that have luminance values of 100% are completely opaque, and those with values between 1% and 99% are semitransparent.

121

31. With the current Composition or Time Layout window as the active window, or with the Composition's name/icon selected in the Project window, go up to your menu bar and select Composition➡Make Movie.

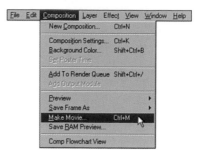

32. A Save Movie As dialog box opens. Save the movie to your desired folder or directory as WriteOn.mov.

122

33. The Render Queue opens next. Here you need to change Render Settings from Current Settings to Best Settings.

34. Next, click on the underlined Output Module setting and change the output module to your choice of format (QuickTime Movie was used in this example). Check Import into project when done so you can quickly see your movie once it's finished rendering.

Output Module Settings

Output Module

Format: QuickTime Movie ▾ ☑ Import into project when done

☑ Video Output

Format Options...

Animation Compressor
Spatial Quality = Most (100)

Channels: RGB + Alpha ▾
Depth: Millions of Colors+ ▾
Color: Premultiplied (With Black) ▾

☐ Stretch

Width   Height

Rendering at: 320   x   240   ☑ Lock Aspect Ratio to (4:3)

Stretch to: 320   x 240   Custom ▾

Stretch %:   x   Stretch Quality: High ▾

☐ Crop

T: 0   L: 0   B: 0   R: 0   Final Size: 320 x 240

☐ Audio Output

Format Options...

44.100 KHz ▾   16 Bit ▾   Stereo ▾

OK   Cancel

35. In the same Output Module Settings dialog box, click on the Format Options button in the Video Output section.

☑ Video Output

Format Options...

Animation Compressor
Spatial Quality = Most (100)

Channels: RGB ▾
Depth: Millions of Colors ▾
Color: Premultiplied (With Black) ▾

☐ Stretch

Width   Height

Rendering at: 320   x   240   ☑ Lock Aspect Ratio to (4:3)

Stretch to: 320   x 240   Custom ▾

Stretch %:   x   Stretch Quality: High ▾

☐ Crop

T: 0   L: 0   B: 0   R: 0   Final Size: 320 x 240

TIP

In this particular project, you're using the Animation codec to save your final tutorial movie. I tried using the Sorenson codec, but it made the movie look so ugly that I couldn't live with it. I affectionately call this process the Compression Threshold of Pain.

36. The Compression Settings dialog box pops up. For this example, choose Animation for your compressor and set it to Best quality. Click OK when you're done.

TIP

If you checked the Import into project when done check box in the Output Module, simply double-click on the movie icon in your Project window.

If you plan to share your project file with others, especially cross-platform, you need to add the .aep extension to your project name.

124

37. When the Render Queue is finally ready, click Render.

After the render is complete, play your movie to make sure it came out the way you expected. If all is well, save your final project as Write-On Text.

The raw artwork supplied for this chapter was created using Discreet 3D Studio MAX.

CHAPTER

7

Creating an Animated Numerical Gauge

You see this technique in use everywhere, from CD-ROM games to animated Web banners. Unfortunately, many times the overall design and execution can be somewhat lacking. A serious designer will pay attention to details like acceleration, deceleration, glows, and the use of blurs.

Numbers have always been an integral part of communication. Scan through just a few TV stations and you'll see numbers encouraging people to call, displaying the price of items, communicating stock values, and so on. Recently, numbers have also become a hip graphical element used in animated designs. Look at just a few of the opening sequences of major motion pictures and you'll find numbers swirling, exploding at the viewer, or randomly flashing as they are communicating the bits and bytes of the digital age.

So what can an animator do to make his or her numbers look their best? Well, one solution is to add effects that help convey the feeling of movement that gives life to your numbers. A Blur is a quick effect that really adds depth and style to any project using animated numbers. Adding a Glow effect reinforces the idea that your numbers are speeding out of control. It's one thing to show numbers changing over time, but it's even better (and a little more work) to make the numbers speed up into a blur and then slow down again near the end. The secret is to set keyframes that create numbers that seem to accelerate and then decelerate. In this chapter, you'll learn precisely when to apply your effects and how to set their keyframes to maximize the idea that you have numbers spinning out of control.

1. Open a new project by clicking File➡New➡New Project.

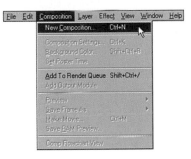

2. Create a new composition by choosing Composition➡New Composition.

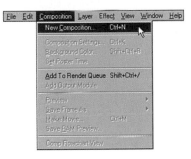

3. In the Composition Settings dialog box, animate your text in a 320×240 composition window because this will be the size of your finished movie. You're going to work at 15 frames per second, with a duration of 5 seconds. Name it Numbers. Click OK when you're done.

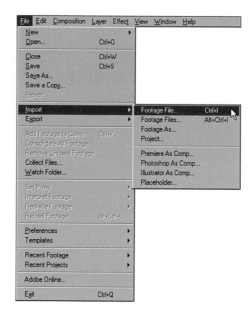

4. To add the video you'll be using, choose File➡Import➡Footage File.

5. Select mech iFace.mov in the Artwork folder for this chapter and click Open.

Open	? X

Look in: 📁 Artwork ▾ 🖿 📷 🏢 🏢

🖹 mech iFace.mov

File name: mech iFace.mov   Open

Files of type: All Formats ▾   Cancel

☐ Sequence not available

6. Drag the mech iFace.mov file from the Project window into the Time Layout window.

Numbers · Time Layout _ □ X

Numbers

0:00:00:00   🔲 **II** **M**

🐵 🔊 🔒   🍥 #   Source Name   🌀 ✳ ↘ ✔ Ⅲ M ⬤   0:00s   01s   02s   03s   04s   05s

🐵   ▷ ☐ 1   📼 mech iFace...   🌀 ◻

◀▶ Switches / Modes   ◀▶ ⚘ △   ⌂ ◁

Now that you've imported the movie file that you plan to use for this project, it's time to create the numbers that will be inset into our animated background (steps 7–12). Now would be a good time to save your project.

7. Create a new solid by going to Layer➡New Solid.

File Edit Composition Layer Effect View Window Help

New Solid...   Ctrl+Y
New Adjustment Layer
Solid Settings...   Shift+Ctrl+Y

Open Effect Controls   Shift+Ctrl+T
Open Layer Window

Mask   ▶
Quality   ▶
Switches   ▶
Transform   ▶
Add Marker

Preserve Transparency
Transfer Mode   ▶
Track Matte   ▶

Bring Layer to Front   Shift+Ctrl+]
Bring Layer Forward   Ctrl+]
Send Layer Backward   Ctrl+[
Send Layer to Back   Shift+Ctrl+[

Toggle Hold Keyframe   Alt+Ctrl+H
Keyframe Interpolation...   Alt+Ctrl+K
Keyframe Velocity...   Shift+Ctrl+K
Keyframe Assistant   ▶

Enable Time Remapping   Alt+Ctrl+T
Time Stretch...
Pre-compose...   Shift+Ctrl+C

129

TIP

As a general rule, it's always a good idea to save your project periodically throughout the creative process. This will save you many headaches in the long run. It's also a good idea to save your project with different names throughout the process (project a, project b, project c, etc.). This way you can go back a few steps if you see that your experimentation has taken you in a different direction than where you want to end up.

TIP

You can also create a new solid by pressing Ctrl+Y on the PC or Cmd+Y on the Mac.

8. Make sure this layer is set at 320×240, and name it Numbers. For now, the color doesn't matter, so click on the OK button.

9. Go to Effect➡Text➡Numbers.

10. The Numbers dialog box opens. Make sure that Direction is set to Horizontal and Alignment is set to Left, and then click the OK button.

11. Place the numbers inside the counter box of your interface by Alt+dragging (or Option+dragging on the Mac) in the Composition window.

12. In the Effect Controls window, adjust the settings for size, tracking, and color, or copy the settings in the screenshot below. Make sure to change Decimal Places to 0.

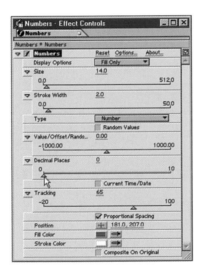

131

In steps 13–23, you'll begin to set keyframes that will animate your numbers. Now would be a good time to save your project.

---

13. Make sure your Current Time Marker is set to the first frame in the Time Layout window.

14. In the Effect Controls window, set the Value/Offset/Random Max amount to 0.

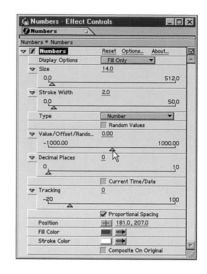

15. Set a keyframe in the Effect Controls window by Alt+clicking (or Option+ clicking on the Mac) on the Value➟Offset➟Random Max setting name.

16. Go to the last frame in the Time Layout window.

17. In the Effect Controls window, click on the Value/Offset/Random Max numeric value so you can give it a numeric value *above* 1000.

18. In the Value/Offset/Random Max settings dialog box that opens, type in 10000 and click OK.

133

19. Move to the 4-second mark in the Time Layout window.

20. Select the Numbers layer and press E to reveal the Numbers effect that has been applied to it. Click on the triangle next to Numbers to reveal all the effect's setting in the Time Layout window.

134

21. Add a keyframe for Value/Offset/Random Max at its current value by clicking the keyframe check box.

22. Repeat step 21 at the 1-second mark in the Time Layout window.

23. Click the triangle next to Value/Offset/Random Max. You now have a nice linear acceleration graph.

NOTE

In After Effects you can control exactly how change occurs between keyframes. The Velocity graph is where you can set your motion to accelerate and decelerate accordingly.

Instead of a nice linear acceleration graph, what you really want is a steeper slope in the middle of the graph, with gentler slopes that gradually form at both ends. In steps 24–29 you'll see just how easy it is to make this happen. Now would be a good time to save your project.

135

24. Pull the keyframe at 1 second up to about 1:15 in the Time Layout window.

Below the Value graph is the Velocity control. You can slide these blackish boxes up or down to affect the acceleration in the graph.

25. Pull the keyframe at 4 seconds down to about 3:10 in the Time Layout window.

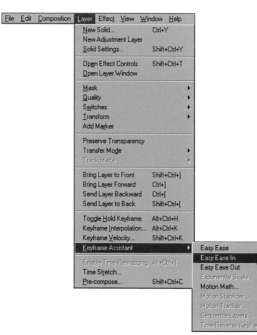

To speed things up, select the desired keyframes and right-click (or Control+click on the Mac) in the Time Layout window. This opens a contextual menu where you can choose Keyframe Assistant (among others). You can then make your selections of Easy Ease Out, Motion Math, etc.

26. Highlight the last keyframe and go to Layer➡Keyframe Assistant➡Easy Ease In.

27. Highlight the second keyframe and go to Layer➡Keyframe Assistant➡ Easy Ease Out.

```
File  Edit  Composition  Layer  Effect  View  Window  Help

                         New Solid...              Ctrl+Y
                         New Adjustment Layer
                         Solid Settings...         Shift+Ctrl+Y

                         Open Effect Controls      Shift+Ctrl+T
                         Open Layer Window

                         Mask                      ▶
                         Quality                   ▶
                         Switches                  ▶
                         Transform                 ▶
                         Add Marker

                         Preserve Transparency
                         Transfer Mode             ▶
                         Track Matte               ▶

                         Bring Layer to Front      Shift+Ctrl+]
                         Bring Layer Forward       Ctrl+]
                         Send Layer Backward       Ctrl+[
                         Send Layer to Back        Shift+Ctrl+[

                         Toggle Hold Keyframe      Alt+Ctrl+H
                         Keyframe Interpolation... Alt+Ctrl+K
                         Keyframe Velocity...      Shift+Ctrl+K
                         Keyframe Assistant        ▶    Easy Ease
                                                        Easy Ease In
                         Enable Time Remapping  Alt+Ctrl+T   Easy Ease Out ⬍
                         Time Stretch...               Exponential Scale
                         Pre-compose...         Shift+Ctrl+C  Motion Math...
                                                        Motion Stabilizer...
                                                        Motion Tracker...
                                                        Sequence Layers
                                                        Time-Reverse Keyframes
```

28. Now the graph should have a more gradual slope.

> **NOTE**
>
> Keyframe Assistants allow you to automatically create and modify keyframes. Although you can create motion in After Effects by setting individual keyframes, Keyframe Assistants automate the process by letting you quickly generate new values for selected properties.

29. Make a RAM preview.

RAM previews are meant to show portions of the composition rather than the entire thing, and how much you'll see depends on how much free RAM you have. For this reason, be sure to temporarily adjust your composition's Work Area Markers before creating a RAM preview. The quickest method is to set the Current Time marker at the desired beginning frame, press the hotkey B, move the marker to the desired ending frame, and press the hotkey N.

With the start point and end point set for the Work Area, there are two methods for creating a RAM preview. You can go to Window, Show Time Controls (or press Ctrl+3 on the PC or Cmd+3 on the Mac) and click the arrow button on the far-right side of the Time Controls box. Or, you can press 0 on your keyboard's numeric keypad.

You may want to collapse the Value and/or Velocity graphs to give yourself more screen real estate.

138

As it is, you have numbers that increase slowly at first, move rapidly through the middle of your composition, and then slow down near the end. You can adjust the overall look by adding keyframes near the ends of the comp, especially near the final frame. In this way, you control the level of acceleration and deceleration. Now would be a good time to save your project.

Now you want the accelerating numbers to heat up. You'll do this in steps 30–37 with a combination of blurs and glows. *Do not worry about the numbers going outside of their interface space.* We will deal with this a little later in the chapter.

30. While the Numbers layer is selected, go to Effect➡Blur & Sharpen➡Fast Blur.

31. Go to the first Value/Offset/Random keyframe and set the Blurriness to 0 and Blur Dimensions to Vertical.

32. Set a keyframe for the blurriness by Alt+clicking (or Option+clicking on the Mac) on the Blurriness control name.

33. Double-click on the second Value/Offset/Random keyframe and change Blurriness to about 11.5.

Slider Control
Blurriness
Minimum value: 0   Maximum value: 32767
Slider Range: [0]   to [127]
Value: [11.5]
[OK]   [Cancel]

34. Move the Current Time marker to about 2 seconds into the comp.

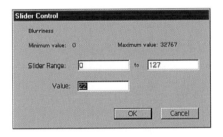

35. Adjust Blurriness to 22.

Slider Control
Blurriness
Minimum value: 0   Maximum value: 32767
Slider Range: [0]   to [127]
Value: [22]
[OK]   [Cancel]

36. Go to about 4:20 and bring the Blurriness down to 0.

Slider Control
Blurriness
Minimum value: 0   Maximum value: 32767
Slider Range: [0]   to [127]
Value: [0]
[OK]   [Cancel]

37. Move back to 4:10 and adjust Blurriness to 25.

Go ahead and make another RAM preview. Now you can really see the effect of the numbers accelerating. The only problem is that they go well outside of the interface space provided. You can fix this by using a mask, as described in steps 38–46. Now would be a good time to save your project.

38. Select the mech iFace layer and duplicate it by going to Edit→Duplicate.

39. Move the new mech iFace layer to the top of the layer stack in Time Layout window.

40. Double-click this layer to open it in its Layer window.

41. Select the Rectangular mask tool.

42. Draw a rectangular mask shape that fits neatly over the space provided for the temperature numbers. Zoom in if you need to.

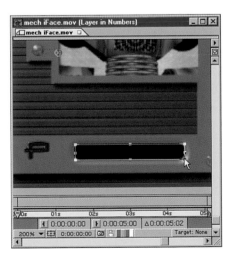

43. Close the Layer window.

TIP

Press the hotkey M while the layer is highlighted to open the layer's Mask Shape property.

142

44. In the Time Layout Window, reveal the Mask property for the top mech iFace.mov layer by clicking the triangle next to the layer name as before.

45. Click the Invert check box.

46. With that done, your numbers will stay in their place in the interface.

47. Reselect the Numbers layer and go to Effect➡Stylize➡Glow.

143

Your numbers are really crankin', so let's heat 'em up in steps 47–53. Specifically, you'll use the Glow effect to give the appearance of heat. You will animate the radius and the intensity of the glow to achieve this look.

48. Accept all the defaults in the Effect Controls Glow box➡except Glow Intensity and Glow Radius, which you should set to 0.

49. Make sure you are at Time Marker 0:00 and set keyframes for both by Alt+clicking (or Option+clicking on the Mac) directly on Glow Intensity and Glow Radius.

50. Double-click the second Value/Offset/Random Max keyframe and adjust Glow Intensity to 1.

Numbers · Effect Controls

Numbers				
Numbers * Numbers				
▷ 🗹 **Numbers**	Reset	Options...	About...	
▷ 🗹 **Fast Blur**	Reset		About...	
▽ 🗹 **Glow**	Reset	Options...	About...	

Glow Based On — Color Channels ▼
Glow Threshold — 60.0%
0.0% — 100.0%
Glow Radius — 0.0
0.0 — 100.0
Glow Intensity — 1.0
0.0 — 4.0
Composite Origin — Behind ▼
Glow Operation — Add ▼
Glow Colors — Original Colors ▼
Color Looping — Triangle A>B>A ▼
Color Loops — 1.0
1.0 — 10.0
Color Phase — 0.0°
A & B Midpoint — 50%
0% — 100%
Color A
Color B
Glow Dimensions — Horizontal and Vertical ▼

You will notice that your numbers look red-hot already, and this probably would be good enough for your effect. But slightly increasing the amount of Glow Radius will improve your effect greatly.

51. Increase Glow Radius to 10.

Slider Control

Glow Radius

Minimum value: 0   Maximum value: 1000

Slider Range: [0] to [100]

Value: [10]

OK   Cancel

52. Go to the 4:00 mark in your Time Layout window and add keyframes for both Radius and Intensity by checking the keyframe check box. You won't change the values here because this will be the beginning of the glow falloff.

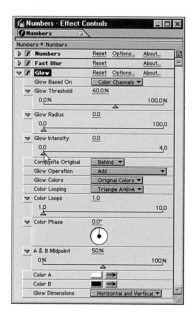

53. Go to the 4:20 mark in your Time Layout window and slide Radius and Intensity to 0.

Now make a RAM preview and check the motion of your text. If it looks the way you want it to, move on to the next steps. If not, go back and tweak some of your parameter settings in the Effect Controls window.

If you're happy with your project after looking at the RAM preview, it's time to render your final movie with all the correct settings for your appropriate output and/or distribution method. Now would be a good time to save your project.

54. With the current Composition or Time Layout window as the active window, or with the composition's name/icon selected in the Project window, go up to your menu bar and select Composition➡Make Movie.

You can also do the Make Movie command by pressing Ctrl+M on the PC or Cmd+M on the Mac.

55. A Save Movie As dialog box opens. Save the movie as TooHot.avi to your desired folder or directory.

147

56. The Render Queue opens next. Here you need to change Render Settings from Current Settings to Best Settings.

57. Next, click on the underlined Output Module setting and change the output module to your choice of format (QuickTime Movie was used in this example). Check "Import into project when done" so you can quickly see your movie when it's finished rendering.

58. In the same Output Module Settings dialog box, click on the Format Options button in the Video Output section.

59. The Compression Settings dialog box pops up. For this example, choose Animation for your compressor and set it at Best Quality. Click OK when done.

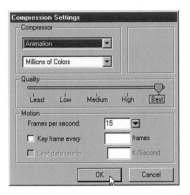

NOTE

In this particular project you are choosing the Animation codec to save your final tutorial movie because I tried using the Sorenson codec and it made the movie look so ugly I couldn't live with the compression. I affectionately call this process the "Compression Threshold of Pain."

60. When the Render Queue is finally ready, click Render.

TIP

If you checked the "Import into project when done" check box in the Output Module, simply double-click on the movie icon in your Project window.

149

TIP

If you plan to share your project file with others, especially cross-platform, you need to add the .aep extension to your project name.

After the render is complete, play your movie to make sure it came out the way you expected. If all is well, save your final project as Accelerated Numbers.99

Part III

Web Effects

The raw artwork supplied for this chapter was created using Adobe Photoshop.

CHAPTER

8

Creating an Animated Web Banner

Animated Web banners are used all over the Net. They drive traffic to sites, introduce new products, sell services, and supply information. Most Web designers will need to create a banner at some point in their careers, even if only to advertise their own services...

Digital Video **Pro's UNITE!**

Designing Web banners has become quite an art form in this new economy. For designers who are used to working with uncompressed, full-resolution video and animation files, working within the proportion constraints and file size limitations of Web banner animation can be rather frustrating at first. After spending so much time worrying about the high quality and resolution of a television commercial, a designer must condense that entire advertising message into an exciting, 8-bit, 468×60, 4-second call to action that immediately sells the product.

Of course, being the animation enthusiast that you are, you'll want to use motion in your Web banner to grab your audience's attention. Unlike other distribution methods, such as film, video, or DVD, you'll want to keep your animation simple and your file size to a minimum. Most commercial Web sites insist that Web banners be no larger than 16KB so that they don't slow down the load time of their pages. In this chapter you'll learn how to build, animate, and save a Web banner from within After Effects.

1. Open a new project by selecting File➡New➡New Project.

2. Import the Photoshop file and all of the graphic layers associated with it by choosing File➡Import➡Photoshop As Comp.

3. Navigate to the Artwork folder for this chapter and select Banner.psd. Click Open.

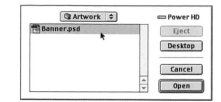

4. You now have two items in your Project window: a folder and a composition, both named Banner.psd. Click on the triangle next to the Banner.psd folder. It now displays the contents of the folder.

154

Now that you've imported the Photoshop file with all eight of its layers, it's time to work with them in the After Effects Time Layout window. You'll be adding motion and effects to specific layers to bring this project to life. Now would be a good time to save your project.

TIP

As a general rule, it's always a good idea to save your project periodically throughout the creative process. This will save you many headaches in the long run. It's also a good idea to save your project with different names throughout the process (project a, project b, project c, etc.). This way you can go back a few steps if you see that your experimentation has taken you in a different direction than where you want to end up.

5. Double-click on the Banner.psd composition at the bottom of your Project window. This will open the Time Layout window and the Composition window.

6. All of the Photoshop layers now appear as composition layers in the After Effects Time Layout window in their correct order.

7. Unfortunately, you can't count on After Effects to keep everything correct. Although it has kept the size correct at 468×60, it will set the frame rate and duration to what you used in your last project. To be on the safe side, go to Composition➡Composition Settings and set Frame Rate to 6 and Duration to 4 seconds. Click OK when you're done.

8. Turn off the visibility of the first six layers by clicking once on each of the Video switch's in the A/V Features panel of the Time Layout window.

155

NOTE

After Effects guessed the correct size we were looking for (468×60) by looking at the size of our imported Photoshop .psd file.

NOTE

If the eye icons are NOT located at the far left of your Time Layout window, then it's because you moved the A/V Features panel. Don't send me email! Just find the icons and go on with your life.

TIP

You can easily turn off the video for all these layers with one click and drag. Click on the top layer's video switch, and drag downward over the 5 below it, turning off each as you go.

9. Select the Arrow layer (layer 7) and press the letter P on your keyboard to reveal the Position parameter control for this layer.

10. With the Time Marker still in place at 0:00, click once on the Position stopwatch icon to set a keyframe.

156

<!---->TIP

Wherever you see an underlined value in After Effects you can click on it to enter the value numerically in a dialog box.

11. Click once on the underlined Position value.

<!---->NOTE

In your Composition window, your white arrow layer should just be appearing on the left side.

12. This opens the Position dialog box. Change X-axis to -35. Make sure that Units is set to pixels. Click OK.

13. Move your Time Marker to the 1-second mark in the Time Layout window.

14. Click once on the Position value (like you did in step 11).

15. Again, this opens the Position dialog box. This time, change X-axis to 90 and click OK.

16. Move your Time Marker to the 2:05-second mark in the Time Layout window.

17. Open the Position dialog box again, change X-axis to 500, and click OK.

Now you're going to start setting the points at which the other layers become visible. The overall design you're presenting is a white arrow that passes a particular area and generates a new word or lights up an existing word. This way, you can take the viewer step-by-step through the message you're trying to convey. Now would be a good time to save your project.

18. Turn on the visibility for layers 2 through 6 by clicking once on each layer's Video switch in the Time Layout window.

19. Select the Digital layer (layer 6).

20. Move your Time Marker to the 10-frame mark in the Time Layout window.

21. Press Option+[on the Mac or Alt+[on the PC to trim your layer's in point to the 10-frame mark.

22. Select the Video layer (layer 5).

23. Move your Time Marker to the 20-frame mark in the Time Layout window.

159

24. Press Option+[on the Mac or Alt+[on the PC to trim your layer's in point to the 20-frame mark.

25. Select the Glow layer (layer 4).

26. Move your Time Marker to the 1-second mark in the Time Layout window.

27. Press Option+[on the Mac or Alt+[on the PC to trim your layer's in point to the 1-second mark.

28. Select the UNITE layer (layer 3).

29. Move your Time Marker to the 1:15-second mark in the Time Layout window.

30. Press Option+[on the Mac or Alt+[on the PC to trim your layer's in point to the 1:15-second mark.

31. Select the !glow layer (layer 2).

162

32. Move your Time Marker to the 2-second mark in the Time Layout window.

33. Press Option+[on the Mac or Alt+[on the PC to trim your layer's in point to the 2-second mark.

34. Press the Spacebar or make a RAM preview to see how the arrow flies across your Web banner, lighting up portions of it along the way.

Now that you've created an interesting animation to attract a Web surfer's eye and send him your message, it's time to reveal who is behind this message and present your call to action. Now would be a good time to save your project.

35. Select the DVPA layer (layer 1).

36. Turn on the visibility for layer 1 by clicking once on the layer's Video switch (like you did in step 18).

37. Move your Time Marker to the 2:10-second mark in the Time Layout window.

38. Press Option+[on the Mac or Alt+[on the PC to trim your layer's in point to the 2:10-second mark.

Make another RAM preview. After the animation is complete, a new graphic appears with the company's logo (or in this example, an association's logo) and the instruction "Click Here".

If you're happy with your project after looking at the RAM preview, it's time to render your final movie with all the correct settings for generating an animated GIF.

39. With the current Composition or Time Layout window as the active window, or with the composition's name/icon selected in the Project window, go up to your menu bar and select Composition➡Make Movie.

40. A Save Movie As dialog box opens. Save the movie as DVPAbanner.gif to your desired folder or directory.

164

41. The Render Queue opens next. Here you need to change Render Settings from Current Settings to Best Settings.

42. Next, click on underlined Output Module setting and change Format to Animated GIF.

43. In the same Output Module Settings dialog box, click on the Format Options button in the Video Output section.

44. In the Animated GIF Options dialog box, you can change the Color Palette, Transparency, Dithering, and Looping options. Accept all of the default settings *except* Dithering, which you should deselect. Click OK when you're done.

TIP
Dithering adds about 25% to the file size of an animated GIF. In this example, it also introduces a lot of noise to your animation. You may want to come back and render the animation with a couple of different combinations of these settings to learn the differences between them and how they affect your images.

45. In the Output Module Settings dialog box, click OK.

46. With the Render Queue finally ready, click Render.

I chose the PICT file format simply because it is a Macintosh standard and this project was developed on a Mac. You may choose whatever format you are most comfortable with and that will import into your preferred Web animation program.

After your render is complete, drag your file into your Web browser to see how it plays.

Although After Effects can produce a decent animated GIF, programs like Adobe ImageReady, Macromedia Fireworks, and GIFBuilder by Yves Piguet can do an even better job. These programs improve performance by optimizing colors, applying individual timing to specific frames, and deleting extra frames that may not be needed.

For this reason, you should also output this animation as a sequence of still images that can be easily imported into any of these programs. You have a lot of still-image sequence options (Tiff, Targa, JPEG, and BMP among them), but for this tutorial you'll use PICT.

47. In the Render Queue window, select Banner.psd under the Comp Name column title.

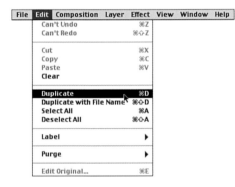

48. Go to Edit➡Duplicate. This will create an exact duplicate of your previous settings.

49. Click once on *Not yet specified* next to the Output To module.

50. This opens the Save As dialog box. Name your new sequence DVPA.pict. Click Save when you're done.

51. Next, click on Based on Lossless and change the Output Module to PICT Sequence.

52. In the Video Output section, there's a new box called Starting #. This allows you to set the first number of the name of the sequence of your stills. Since there aren't too many people who begin counting at zero, change the first number to 1. Click OK to get back to the Render Queue.

53. Notice that your Output To module now reads DVPA...[#####].pict. This reflects the sequential numbering that will be applied to your PICT sequence automatically. When the Render Queue is finally ready, click Render.

After the render is complete, you will have created 24 individual images, numbered sequentially, that you can now easily import into a Web optimization program. You'll find that the last image can have a 1.5-second hold applied to it, and that the previous eight images (representing frames) can be thrown away. This can all be done in your Web optimization program and will further optimize your file size. If you look inside the Final Movie folder for this chapter on the CD, you'll find a folder named After ImageReady with an optimized version of this Web banner animation that was created using this PICT sequence of images.

Save the final version of this project as Web Banner.

TIP

If you plan to share your project file with others, especially cross-platform, you need to add the .aep extension to your project name.

169

Part IV

Video Effects

The raw artwork supplied for this chapter was created using Discreet 3D Studio MAX. You'll need the Production Bundle version of After Effects to complete this tutorial.

CHAPTER

9

Giving Animation a Handheld Camcorder Look

Please note that no babies were harmed in the making of this project.

In this chapter, you'll look at a way of giving your video, graphics, or computer animations that natural/amateur look that has become so popular recently. The problem with computer-generated images is that they can be so pristine that they seem fake or unnatural. With this technique, you'll give your movie clip a camcorder feel.

For this project, let's make believe that one of your clients is a company that makes diapers. This client wants to launch a new promotional campaign to convince the audience that these diapers are superior to the competition because they're specially tested in ultra-tough real-world conditions. To prove this point, your client has hired babies trained in the martial arts and videotaped them in action to demonstrate the flexibility, durability, and comfort-fit of these hi-tech diapers. The babies were outstanding; the diapers were flawless. The only problem is that the video looks a bit flat for the client's tastes, and his schedule won't allow him to return to the top-secret baby kumite testing grounds in time to get this spot out to broadcast. So your client has asked you to give the video a "handheld" feel.

You could do this by keyframing the video as you manually moved it around in the Composition window. This usually requires a lot of preplanning to avoid excessive jerkiness or a mechanical motion. You'll also need a whole lot of keyframes to give it sufficient "jitter." The final results are bound to be unsatisfactory, unrealistic, and unpredictable.

The best method is to use two of After Effects' plug-ins, the Wiggler and the Smoother. (Adobe doesn't spend a lot of time on names, apparently.) By placing only four keyframes manually, you'll make the video look like it was shot by an excited spectator at the Baby Kumite Ultimate Fighting Championship.

1. Open a new project by clicking File➡New➡New Project.

2. Create a new composition by choosing Composition➡New Composition.

TIP

You can also create a new composition by pressing Ctrl+N on the PC or Cmd+N on the Mac.

3. In the Composition Settings dialog box, animate your text in a 320×240 composition window because this will be the size of your finished movie. You're going to work at 15 frames per second, with a duration of 7 seconds. Name it Handheld Vidcam. Click OK when you're done.

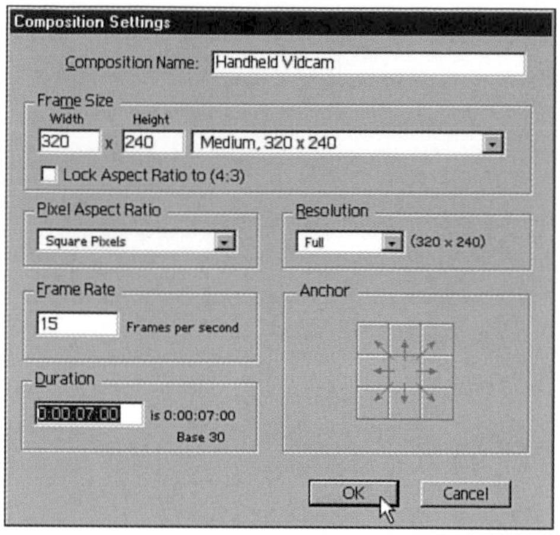

4. To add the video you will be using, choose File→Import→Footage File.

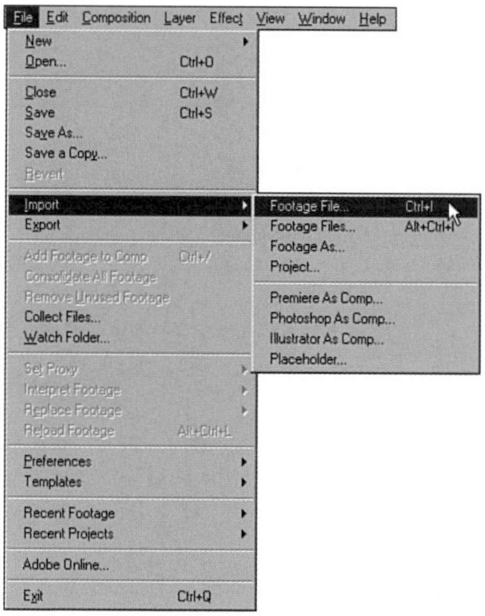

TIP

You can also import footage by doing the following:

PC—Right-click in the project window, or press Ctrl+I.
Mac—Hold down the Ctrl key and click in the project window, or press Cmd+I.

Or you can simply double-click inside the Project window in the white area (*not* on a file).

5. Now select baby kumite.mov in the Artwork folder for the chapter.

Now that you've imported the movie file that you plan to use for this project, it's time to move it from the Project window to the Time Layout window. Now would be a good time to save your project.

6. Place the baby kumite video layer in the Time Layout window, which automatically centers it in the Composition window.

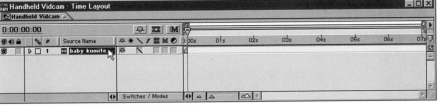

175

7. Click on the triangle to the left of the layer's name. This reveals the properties for this layer that can be animated.

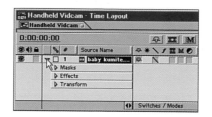

8. Click on Transform to reveal additional values.

176

9. Click on the underlined Scale percentage to enter a new Scale value.

TIP

Press the S hotkey while the layer is selected to reveal the Scale property. The other hotkeys you'll be using for this project are R for revealing rotation and P for revealing position.

10. Enter a new Scale value of 110% and click OK.

Trying to simulate jerky handheld motions using traditional keyframing techniques would make you quit your job. Luckily, After Effects provides tools that can accomplish this for you automatically. With just a few clicks, you can instantly create hundreds of keyframes. You'll learn how to work with the Wiggler in steps 11–17.

11. Reveal the Rotation property by pressing R. At the first frame of the composition, set a keyframe for Rotation by clicking on the stopwatch to the left.

TIP

Use the hotkeys Alt+R on the PC or Opt+R on the Mac to set a keyframe at the current value.

12. After Effects will be doing most of the work for you, so leave the Rotation value at 0.0.

177

NOTE

If the keyframe checkbox isn't located at the far left of your Time Layout window, it's because you've changed your default settings. Look around your Time Layout window and I'm sure you'll find it.

13. Go to the final frame of the composition. Click in the Keyframe check box to the far left of Rotation to set a second keyframe. Again, there's no need to adjust the value.

14. Highlight both Rotation keyframes by clicking on Rotation in the Time Layout window.

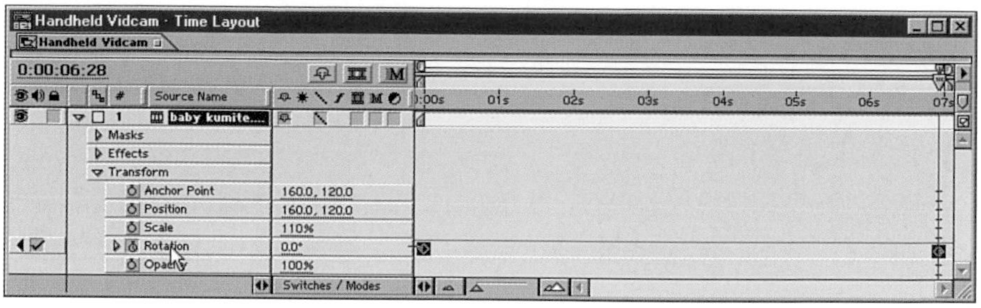

15. Select Window, Plug-in Palettes, The Wiggler. The Wiggler does just what its name implies: It wiggles values. In this case it's going to create random keyframes for your layer's rotation.

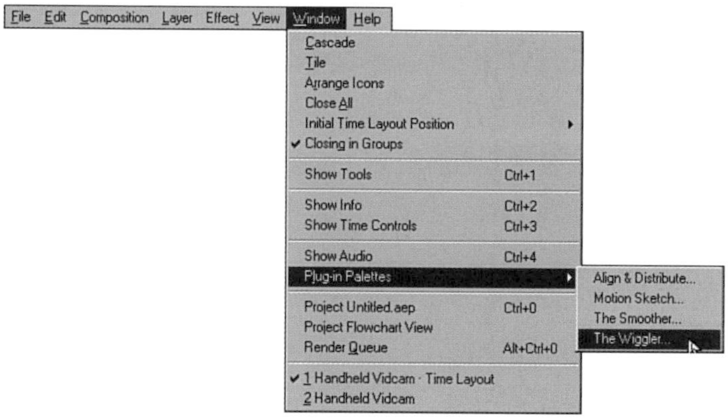

16. You control the amount of wiggle in the Wiggler's settings box. You can spend hours playing with all the different combinations to get just the right look you're after. In the interest of time, duplicate the settings in the following figure and click Apply.

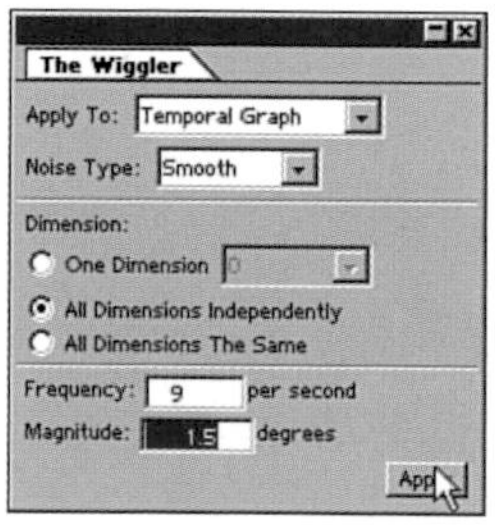

17. The Time Layout window shows the new Rotation keyframes.

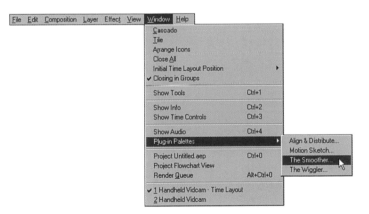

The first time you do this, you *are* allowed to say "Whoa, cool!" But by the second time, this is frowned upon in professional circles.

Of course, such a high number of keyframes means more computations, which ultimately means longer render times. Don't fret; there *is* a simple way to shorten your render time. It's a wonderful plug-in called the Smoother, and in steps 18–21 you'll see how it removes unnecessary keyframes while keeping the overall animation. Now would be a good time to save your project.

18. Make sure that your new keyframes are still selected, and then go to Window➡Plug-in Palettes➡The Smoother.

TIP

If the keyframes are no longer selected, click on Rotation again to reselect them.

19. Duplicate the settings for the Smoother in following figure and then click Apply.

180

20. The Time Layout window shows the reduced number of keyframes.

21. Make a RAM preview and notice the wiggle in your video.

Simply by creating two keyframes and applying AE's Keyframe Assistants without manually changing any values, you've quickly created a smooth, fully animated sequence consisting of approximately 30 keyframes of varying values. Pat yourself on the back; you're working like a pro now. Now would be a good time to save.

However, to finish the handheld look, you now need to apply the Wiggler and the Smoother to your Position keyframes.

22. Repeat steps 11–15 for the layer's Position keyframes.

23. Use the same Wiggler settings as in step 16, except now they'll be applied to the Spatial Path. (Thankfully, the settings haven't returned to their defaults!)

NOTE

Spatial Path is automatically selected for you because you're applying the Wiggler to the Spatial property position.

NOTE

Spatial Path adds deviations to your motion, while Temporal Graph adds deviations to your velocity.

NOTE

If you're not happy with the effect, go back and experiment with the settings used in the Wiggler. First, select all the keyframes in either Rotation or Position, as described previously. Then adjust the values in the Wiggler's settings box and apply. Don't forget to use the Smoother while the new keyframes are still selected.

TIP

You can also execute the Make Movie command by pressing Ctrl+M on the PC or Cmd+M on the Mac.

24. Repeat steps 18 and 19. This time, the Smoother is also applied to the Spatial Path.

Make another RAM preview. If you're happy with the handheld effect, it's time to render your final movie with all the correct settings for your appropriate output and/or distribution method. Now would be a good time to save your project.

---

25. With the current Composition or Time Layout window as the active window, or with the composition's name/icon selected in the Project window, go up to your menu bar and select Composition➡Make Movie.

26. A Save Movie As dialog box will open. Save the movie to your desired folder or directory as Handheld Vidcam.

27. The Render Queue opens next. Here you need to change Render Settings from Current Settings to Best Settings.

28. Next, click on the underlined Output Module setting and change the output module to your choice of format (QuickTime Movie was used in this example). Check Import into project when done so you can quickly see your movie once it's finished rendering.

Output Module Settings

Output Module

Format: QuickTime Movie ▾ ☑ Import into project when done

☑ Video Output

Format Options...

Animation Compressor
Spatial Quality = High (92)

Channels: RGB ▾
Depth: Millions of Colors ▾
Color: Premultiplied (With Black) ▾

☐ Stretch

Width   Height

Rendering at: 320   x   240   ☑ Lock Aspect Ratio to (4:3)

Stretch to: 320   x 240   Custom ▾

Stretch %:   x   Stretch Quality: High ▾

☐ Crop

T: 0   L: 0   B: 0   R: 0   Final Size: 320 x 240

☐ Audio Output

Format Options...

44.100 KHz ▾   16 Bit ▾   Stereo ▾

OK   Cancel

29. In the same Output Module Settings dialog box, click on the Format Options button in the Video Output section.

☑ Video Output

Format Options...

Animation Compressor
Spatial Quality = High (92)

Channels: RGB ▾
Depth: Millions of Colors ▾
Color: Premultiplied (With Black) ▾

☐ Stretch

Width   Height

Rendering at: 320   x   240   ☑ Lock Aspect Ratio to (4:3)

Stretch to: 320   x 240   Custom ▾

Stretch %:   x   Stretch Quality: High ▾

☐ Crop

T: 0   L: 0   B: 0   R: 0   Final Size: 320 x 240

30. The Compression Settings dialog box pops up. For this example, choose Sorenson Video as your compressor and set it to Best Quality. Click OK when you're done.

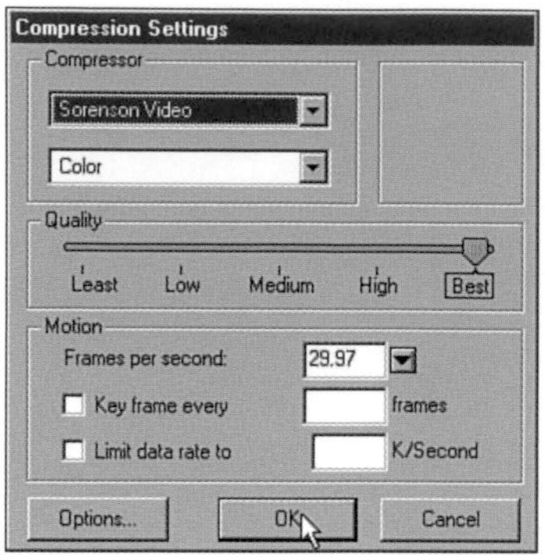

31. When the Render Queue is finally ready, click Render.

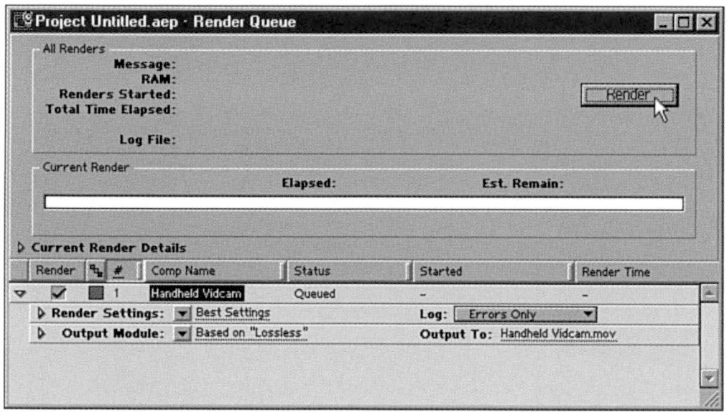

184

TIP

If you checked the Import into project when done check box in the Output Module, simply double-click on the movie icon in your Project window.

TIP

If you plan to share your project file with others, especially cross-platform, you need to add the .aep extension to your project name.

Place your bets on baby number 1. He's tough.

After the render is complete, play your movie to make sure it came out the way you expected. If all is well, save your final project as Handheld Vidcam.

*The video clip supplied for this chapter was obtained from the Exploring Space Royalty Free Stock Footage collection from Dynamic Graphics (**http://www.dgusa.com**).*

CHAPTER
10 Quick and Easy Promo Creation

This technique is used more often than people realize, especially in television commercials. Many times you see this technique applied in slow motion so that viewers can examine the devastating effect of a car crash or other disaster.

This project will reveal the magic behind a couple of the most commonly requested tricks used in post-production. The first trick is revealing text with a lens flare effect. This look is commonly requested by clients who want to surprise their audience by suddenly revealing a new logo or the new name of a product. Although there are third-party plug-ins that can easily re-create this effect, you'll learn how to use the standard version of After Effects, along with transparency modes, to save some of your hard-earned money. That's why you bought this book, isn't it?

The second trick is reversing video in After Effects. If you haven't already done so, at some point in your After Effects career you're going to scream out, "Hey! Where's the Make My Video Go Backwards button?" It seems like making video run backwards would be the simplest thing in the world to do. And it is. But if you don't know the trick (the most important keyboard shortcut in AE), you might spend an hour or more trying different ways to switch the start and end points of your layer. Sometimes something simple can quickly become very frustrating. This project will show you an easy way to make your video run in reverse with exceptional quality.

1. Open a new project by clicking File→New→New Project.

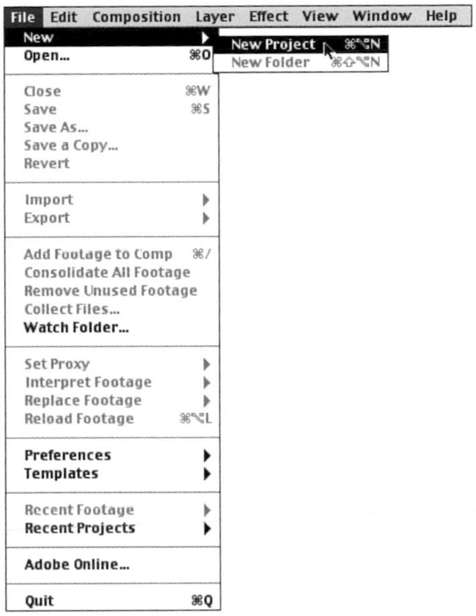

| File | Edit | Composition | Layer | Effect | View | Window | Help |

New... ▶
Open... ⌘O

New Project ⌘⌥N
New Folder ⌘⇧⌥N

Close ⌘W
Save ⌘S
Save As...
Save a Copy...
Revert

Import ▶
Export ▶

Add Footage to Comp ⌘/
Consolidate All Footage
Remove Unused Footage
Collect Files...
Watch Folder...

Set Proxy ▶
Interpret Footage ▶
Replace Footage ▶
Reload Footage ⌘⌥L

Preferences ▶
Templates ▶

Recent Footage ▶
Recent Projects ▶

Adobe Online...

Quit ⌘Q

2. To add the video file you will be using in this project, choose File→Import→Footage File.

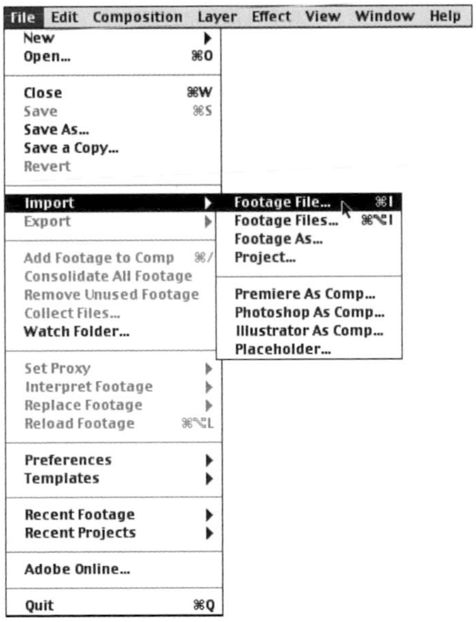

| File | Edit | Composition | Layer | Effect | View | Window | Help |

New ▶
Open... ⌘O

Close ⌘W
Save ⌘S
Save As...
Save a Copy...
Revert

Import ▶
Export ▶

Footage File... ⌘I
Footage Files... ⌘⌥I
Footage As...
Project...

Premiere As Comp...
Photoshop As Comp...
Illustrator As Comp...
Placeholder...

Add Footage to Comp ⌘/
Consolidate All Footage
Remove Unused Footage
Collect Files...
Watch Folder...

Set Proxy ▶
Interpret Footage ▶
Replace Footage ▶
Reload Footage ⌘⌥L

Preferences ▶
Templates ▶

Recent Footage ▶
Recent Projects ▶

Adobe Online...

Quit ⌘Q

TIP

187

You can also import footage by doing the following:

PC—Right-click in the project window, or press Ctrl+I.
Mac—Hold down the Ctrl key and click in the project window, or press Cmd+I.

Or you can simply double-click inside the Project window in the white area (*not* on a file).

3. Now select Space Station.mov in the Artwork folder for this chapter. Click OK when you're done.

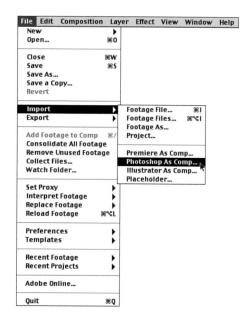

4. You also need to import a couple of text layers for use with this project. To import the Photoshop file and all of the graphic layers associated with it, choose File➡Import➡Photoshop As Comp.

5. The dialog box should open to the Artwork folder for this chapter (since you just chose another file from this location). Select MIR text.psd and click Open.

6. You now have three items in your Project window: a folder and a composition that are both named MIR text.psd, and a video file named Space Station.mov. Click on the triangle next to the folder named MIR text.psd. Notice how it displays the contents of the folder.

You'll work with the imported Photoshop composition first. You'll be adding motion and effects to key layers to bring this project to life. Now would be a good time to save your project.

7. Double-click on the MIR text.psd composition in your Project window. This will open the Time Layout window and the Composition window.

189

8. All of the Photoshop layers have been transferred over to the After Effects Time Layout window in their correct order.

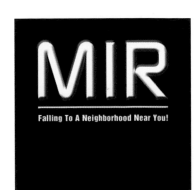

190

NOTE

The Composition size is based on the size of the original Photoshop file.

9. Unfortunately, you can't count on After Effects to keep everything correct. Although it keeps the size correct at 320×240, it will set the frame rate and duration to what you used in your last project. To be on the safe side, go to Composition➡Composition Settings.

10. Set the Frame Rate to 29.97 and the Duration to 7 seconds. Click OK when you're done.

NOTE

If the eye icons aren't located at the far left of your Time Layout window, it's because you moved the A/V Features panel.

11. In the Time Layout window, turn off the visibility of layer 2 by clicking once on the layer's Video Switch (eye icon) at the left side of the window.

In steps 12–26 you'll animate the revealing of your text. While there are a number of ways to do this, one of the simplest is to apply a Linear Wipe. Specifically, you will animate the wipe on the screen moving from left to right.

12. Select the MIR layer (layer 1).

13. Move your Time Marker to the 3-second mark in the Time Layout window.

14. Press Option+[on the Mac or Alt+[on the PC to trim your layer start point to the 3-second mark.

15. Go to Effect➡Transition➡Linear Wipe.

16. Press the letter E on your keyboard to reveal the Effect Parameter settings (in this case Linear Wipe) in the Time Layout window.

17. Click once on the Linear Wipe triangle to expose the settings.

18. Click once on the underlined Feather numeric value.

```
┌──────────────────────────────────────────────┐
│ □                                 MIR text.ps  │
│ ┌─────────────────────────────────────────┐   │
│ │ MIR text.psd                            │   │
│ │ 0;00;03;00                      🔲 🔲 M  │   │
│ │ 🔊 🔒   📋 #  Layer Name      🔲 ✳ ＼ ✎ ▦ M ◎│
│ │ 🔲   ▽ □ 1   🔳 MIR            🔲   ＼ ✎ │   │
│ │ ✎       ▽ Linear Wipe          Reset    │   │
│ │           ⏱ Transition Completion  0%   │   │
│ │           ⏱ Wipe Angle         90.0°    │   │
│ │           ⏱ Feather            0.0      │   │
│ │       ▷ □ 2  🔳 Falling to a...  🔲 ▪ ＼ │   │
│ │                                 🔲 Switches / Modes │
│ └─────────────────────────────────────────┘   │
└──────────────────────────────────────────────┘
```

19. This opens the Feather Control dialog box. Change Value to 75 and click OK.

```
┌──────────────────────────────────────────┐
│ ═══════════ Slider Control ═══════════    │
│                                           │
│  Feather                                  │
│                                           │
│  Minimum value: 0      Maximum value: 32000│
│                                           │
│  Slider Range: [    0   ] to [   100   ]  │
│                                           │
│        Value: [   75   ]                  │
│                                           │
│                    [ Cancel ]  [  OK  ]   │
└──────────────────────────────────────────┘
```

20. Click once on the underlined Wipe Angle numeric value.

```
┌──────────────────────────────────────────────┐
│ □                                 MIR text.ps  │
│ ┌─────────────────────────────────────────┐   │
│ │ MIR text.psd                            │   │
│ │ 0;00;03;00                      🔲 🔲 M  │   │
│ │ 🔊 🔒   📋 #  Layer Name      🔲 ✳ ＼ ✎ ▦ M ◎│
│ │ 🔲   ▽ □ 1   🔳 MIR            🔲   ＼ ✎ │   │
│ │ ✎       ▽ Linear Wipe          Reset    │   │
│ │           ⏱ Transition Completion  0%   │   │
│ │           ⏱ Wipe Angle         90.0°    │   │
│ │           ⏱ Feather            75.0     │   │
│ │       ▷ □ 2  🔳 Falling to a...  🔲 ＼   │   │
│ │                                 🔲 Switches / Modes │
│ └─────────────────────────────────────────┘   │
└──────────────────────────────────────────────┘
```

21. This opens the Wipe Control dialog box. Change Degrees to 270 and click OK.

```
┌──────────────────────────────────────────┐
│ ═══════════ Angle Control ═══════════     │
│                                           │
│  Wipe Angle                               │
│                                           │
│      Revolutions    Degrees               │
│      [    0    ]  + [   270   ]  (positive is clockwise)│
│                                           │
│                    [ Cancel ]  [  OK ▶ ]  │
└──────────────────────────────────────────┘
```

22. Make sure you're at the 3:00 Time Marker. Then click once on the Transition Completion stopwatch icon to set a keyframe.

23. Click once on the Transition Completion numeric value.

24. This opens the Transition Completion Control dialog box. Change Value to 100 and click OK.

25. Move your Time Marker to the 4-second mark in the Time Layout window.

26. Again, click on the Transition Completion numeric value to open the Slider Control dialog box, and then change Value to 0. Click OK when you're done.

```
                      Slider Control
  Transition Completion
  Minimum value: 0              Maximum value: 100

  Slider Range:    0        to        100

  Value:          0

                              Cancel      OK ▶
```

Create a RAM preview to see what you've accomplished so far. Now that you've set the way that the text is going to appear onscreen, it's time to add a little illusion. You'll add a lens flare effect so that it looks like the words are appearing as the lens flare flies across the screen. Now would be a good time to save your project.

27. Move the Time Marker to the 3-second mark.

```
                              MIR text.psd • Time Layout
  MIR text.psd
  0;00;03;00                    ⊕ ▯▯ ▯
  ⊗ ◀)) ▯   %  #  Layer Name    ⊕ * \ ƒ ▤ ▥ ◉  :00s  01s  02s  03s  04s  05s  06s  07s
  ⊗     ▽ ▯ 1  ▯ MIR            ⊕   \ ƒ
  ƒ        ▽ Linear Wipe        Reset
  ✓ ▶        ▷ ◉ Transition Completion  100%
               ◉ Wipe Angle     270.0°
               ◉ Feather        75.0
           ▷ ▯ 2  ▯ Falling to a...  ⊕   \
                              ◀▶  Switches / Modes   ◀▶ ▵ ▵    ▵            ◀ ▶
```

28. Create a new layer by going to Layer➡New Solid.

```
  File  Edit  Composition  Layer  Effect  View  Window  Help
                           New Solid...              ⌘Y
                           New Adjustment Layer
                           Solid Settings...          ⌘⇧Y

                           Open Effect Controls       ⌘⇧T
                           Open Layer Window

                           Mask                     ▶
                           Quality                  ▶
                           Switches                 ▶
                           Transform                ▶
                           Add Marker

                           Preserve Transparency
                           Transfer Mode            ▶
                           Track Matte              ▶

                           Bring Layer to Front      ⌘⇧]
                           Bring Layer Forward        ⌘]
                           Send Layer Backward        ⌘[
                           Send Layer to Back        ⌘⇧[

                           Toggle Hold Keyframe     ⌘⌥H
                           Keyframe Interpolation...  ⌘⌥K
                           Keyframe Velocity...      ⌘⇧K
                           Keyframe Assistant       ▶

                           Enable Time Remapping     ⌘⌥T
                           Time Stretch...
                           Pre-compose...            ⌘⇧C
```

195

NOTE

RAM previews are meant to show portions of the composition rather than the entire thing, and how much you see depends on how much free RAM you have. For this reason, be sure to temporarily adjust your composition's work area markers before creating a RAM preview. The quickest method is to set the Current Time marker at the desired beginning, press the hotkey B, move the marker to the desired end, and press the hotkey N.

With the beginning and end Work Area markers set, there are two methods to create a RAM preview. Go to Window, Show Time Controls (or press Ctrl+3 on the PC or Cmd+3 on the Mac) and click the arrow button on the far right of the Time Controls box. Or, press 0 on your keyboard's numeric keypad.

TIP

If you hold down the Shift key while making a RAM preview, After Effects will only cache *every other frame*. This trick can be a huge timesaver, especially if the only reason you're making a RAM preview is to check the basic motion of your layers.

TIP

You can also create a new solid by pressing Ctrl+Y on the PC or Cmd+Y on the Mac.

29. Make sure this layer is set to 320×240 and the color is set to black. Name it Flare and click on the OK button.

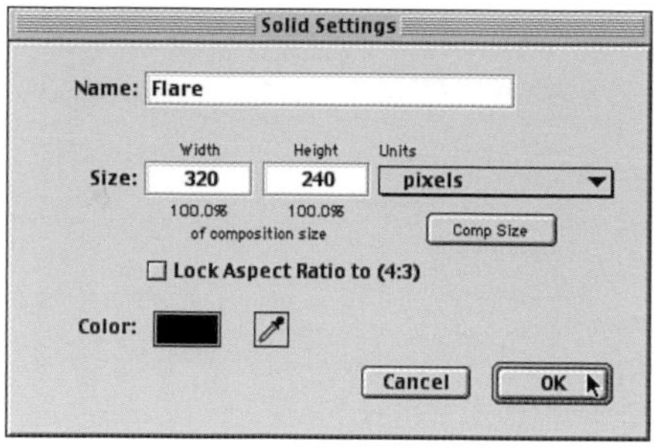

30. Add the lens flare to this Solid layer by going to Effect➡Render➡ PS+ Lens Flare.

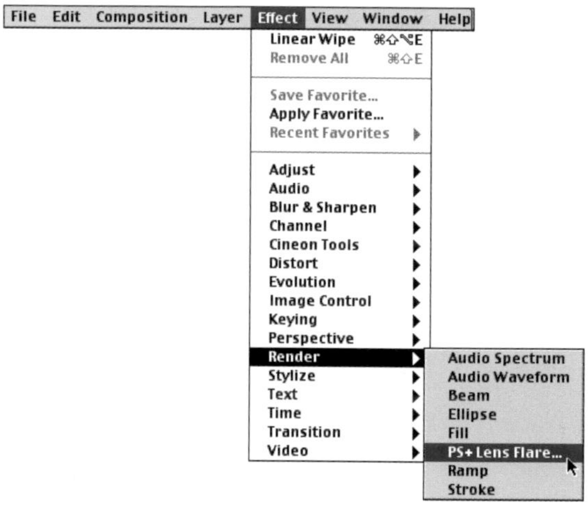

196

NOTE

The three Lens Flare options show what a lens flare would look like if it appeared through various lens types:

50–300mm zoom imitates a zoom lens.

35mm prime imitates a wide-angle lens.

105mm prime imitates a telephoto lens.

31. The Lens Flare options dialog box pops up. Make sure that Lens type is 50–300mm zoom, and then click OK.

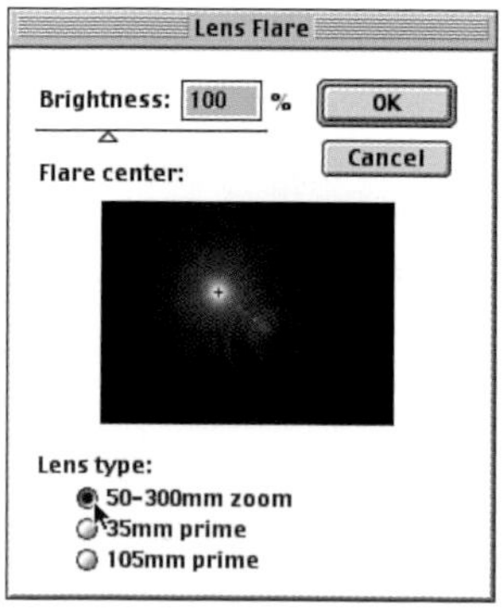

32. In the Effect Controls window, click on the underlined numeric value for Flare Brightness.

33. This opens the Flare Brightness dialog box. Change Value to 160 and click OK.

34. Now click on the X,Y coordinates for Flare Center.

35. This opens the Flare Center dialog box. Change X-axis to 0 and Y-axis to 100. Click OK when you're done.

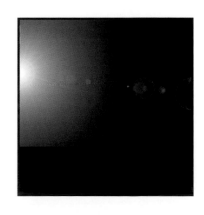

36. To set a keyframe for this property, hold down the Option key on the Mac or the Alt key on the PC while clicking once on Flare Center.

37. Move the Time Marker to the 4-second mark.

38. Once again, click on the X,Y coordinates for Flare Center.

39. This opens the Flare Center dialog box. Change X-axis to 435 and leave Y-axis set to 100. Click OK when you're done.

40. To allow the MIR text layer to show through the Flare layer, you need to change the layer's Transfer mode. Click once on the Switches/Modes button at the bottom of the Time Layout window.

41. On the Flare layer (layer 1), change the Transfer Mode from Normal to Screen.

Make a RAM preview. Notice how the Lens Flare covers up the Linear Wipe to create the illusion of the MIR text being written by light. You've animated the Flare Center of the Lens Flare to closely match the Linear Wipe that's revealing your MIR text. Now you'll bring in the tag line with a simple, understated dissolve. Now would be a good time to save your project.

---

42. Select the layer called Falling to a... (layer 3) in the Time Layout window.

43. Turn on the visibility of layer 3 by clicking once on the layer's Video Switch (eye icon) at the left side of the window.

44. Move your Time Marker to the 6-second mark in the Time Layout window.

45. Press the letter T on your keyboard to reveal Opacity for this layer.

TIP

You can also set an Opacity keyframe by pressing Opt+T on the Mac (Alt+Shift+T on the PC).

46. Click once on the Opacity stopwatch icon to set a keyframe at the current value of 100%.

47. Move your Time Marker to the 5-second mark in the Time Layout window.

48. Click once on the underlined Opacity numeric value.

49. This opens the Opacity settings dialog box. Change the value to 0% and click OK.

50. Press Option+[on the Mac or Alt+[on the PC to trim your layer in point to the 5-second mark.

Now that you've created all of the text effects that will be used in the project, it's time to create a composition to hold your space station footage and your new MIR text composition. You'll also be reversing the playback direction of your space station clip. Now would be a good time to save your project.

51. Create a new composition by choosing Composition➡New Composition.

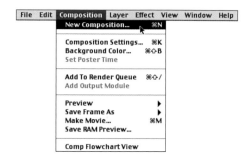

52. In the Composition Settings dialog box, animate your text in a 320×240 composition window because this will be the size of your finished movie. You're going to work at 29.97 frames per second, with a duration of 7 seconds. Name it Emit. ("Time" backwards—corny, huh?) Click OK when you're done.

53. Drag Space Station.mov from the Project window to the Time Layout window.

54. Press the spacebar on your keyboard to play the video clip. Notice how it starts with a wide-angle view of the space station and then narrows to a close-up.

204

55. Press Cmd+Opt+R on the Mac or Ctrl+Alt+R on the PC to reverse the playback direction of your video clip. Notice the stripes that now appear on your layer's duration bar in the Time Layout window.

That's it. Your video is now running in reverse. Notice that you now have a video clip that starts with a close-up and pulls out to a wide shot. It's like having your own video director in outer space! Now go show your friends that you've learned how to turn back time, just like Superman.

The last few steps simply combine your MIR text composition with your reversed video clip. Now would be a good time to save your project.

56. Make sure your Time Marker is at 0.00 in the Time Layout window, and then drag the composition (*not* the folder) named MIR text.psd from the Project window to the Time Layout window.

57. To allow the MIR text.psd layer to appear on top of the space station.mov layer, you need to change Transfer mode. Click once on the Switches/Modes button at the bottom of the Time Layout window.

58. On the MIR text.psd layer (layer 1), change the Transfer Mode from Normal to Screen.

Make a RAM preview. If you're happy with your project after looking at the RAM preview, it's time to render your final movie with all the correct settings for your appropriate output and/or distribution method.

59. With the current Composition or Time Layout window as the active window, or with the composition's name/icon selected in the Project window, go up to your menu bar and select Composition➡Make Movie.

TIP

You can also do the Make Movic command by pressing Ctrl+M on the PC or Cmd+M on the Mac.

205

60. A Save Movie As dialog box opens. Save the movie as Emit to your desired folder or directory.

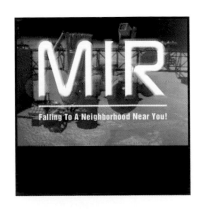

61. The Render Queue will open next. Here you need to change Render Settings from Current Settings to Best Settings.

62. Next, click on the underlined Output Module setting and change the output module to your choice of format (QuickTime Movie was used in this example). Check Import into project when done so you can quickly see your movie once it's finished rendering.

63. In the same Output Module Settings dialog box, click on the Format Options button in the Video Output section.

64. The Compression Settings dialog box pops up. For this example, choose Sorenson for your compressor and set it to Best Quality. Click OK twice to get back to the Render Queue.

207

TIP

If you checked the Import into project when done check box in the Output Module, simply double-click on the movie icon in your Project window.

TIP

If you plan to share your project file with others, especially cross-platform, you need to add the .aep extension to your project name.

65. When the Render Queue is finally ready, click Render.

After the render is complete, play your movie to make sure it came out the way you expected. If all is well, save your final project as Emit.

Part V

Background Effects

The raw artwork supplied for this chapter was created using Adobe Photoshop.

CHAPTER
11

Making a Waving Flag from a Still Photo

Although this technique uses rudimentary graphics to show off its simplicity, a multilayered graphic, animation, or video file could be used to add even more stunning results.

It seems like a simple request for a project: Take a still image of a flag and make it flutter in an imaginary breeze. After Effects has a plug-in for that, right? Well, there's the Displacement filter, but it makes the flag move about like it's swimming in the ocean. Oops. I don't think the client is going to pay for that.

A little bit of tinkering is required with a program as multifaceted as After Effects. After a few dead ends and some sugar breaks, you can discover the right combination of tools and layering. But who wants to go through all that? Here are the steps to make a flag flutter in the wind the way it's supposed to (and the way the client wants).

1. Open a new project by clicking File➡New➡New Project.

2. Create a new composition by choosing Composition➡New Composition.

> **TIP**
>
> You can also create a new composition by pressing Ctrl+N on the PC or Cmd+N on the Mac.

3. In the New Composition dialog box, animate your text in a 320×240 composition window because this will be the size of your finished movie. You're going to work at 15 frames per second, with a duration of 5 seconds. Name it Flag. Click OK when you're done.

TIP

You can also import multiple footage files by pressing Ctrl+Alt+I on the PC or Cmd+ Option+I on the Mac.

4. To add the images you'll be using, choose File➡Import➡Footage Files.

5. Navigate to the Artwork folder for this chapter and select FLA flag.psd. Click Open.

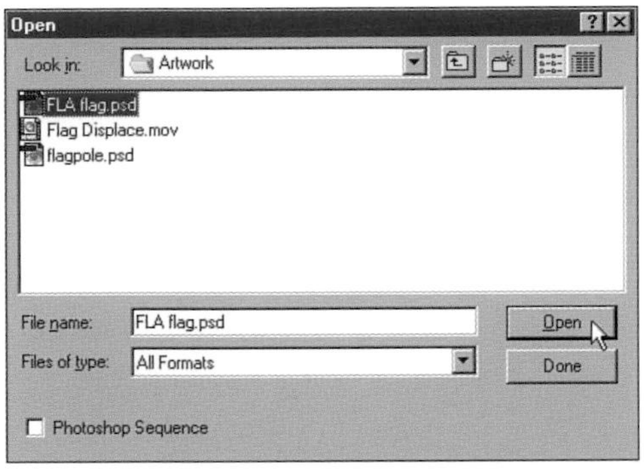

6. The Import dialog box will remain open. This time, select flagpole.psd. Click Open.

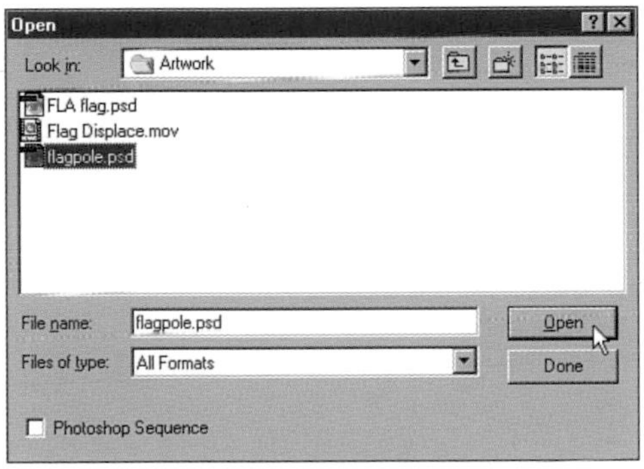

NOTE

If you get the Interpret Footage dialog box after selecting flagpole.psd, choose Treat as Straight (Unmatted) and click OK to continue with the tutorial.

213

7. The Import dialog box will remain open. This time, select Flag Displace.mov. Click Open, and then click Done.

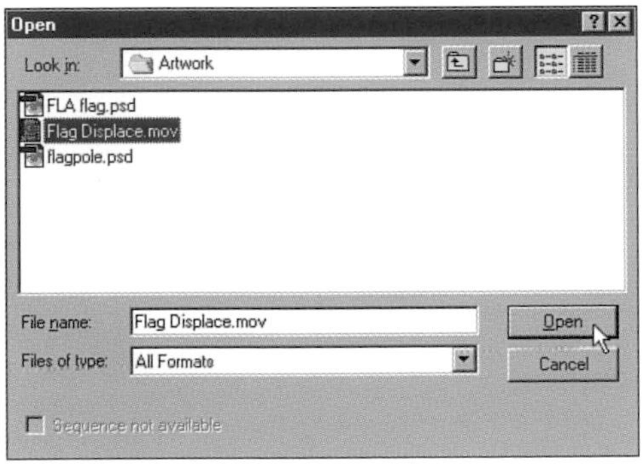

TIP

As a general rule, it's always a good idea to save your project periodically throughout the creative process. This will save you many headaches in the long run. It's also a good idea to save your project with different names throughout the process (project a, project b, project c, etc.). This way you can go back a few steps if you see that your experimentation has taken you in a different direction than where you want to end up.

Now that you've imported the movie file that you plan to use for this project, it's time to move it from the Project window to the Time Layout window. Now would be a good time to save your project.

8. Place FLA flag.PSD, flagpole.PSD, and Flag Displace.MOV (in this order)in the Time Layout window so that FLA flag.psd is on top.

9. Scale down the flag,psd layer to 70%. Don't worry if it isn't in the exact right spot. You'll fix this later. Click OK when done.

214

NOTE

You are increasing the layer's size by placing the scaled-down layer in a larger composition, thus giving it more room to move so that the edges aren't cut off. This is why you are pre-composing.

You want one end of the flag to seem tied down on the flagpole and the opposite end to flap in the wind. To give it a more free-flowing effect, you need to give it more room to flap. You'll do this by pre-composing.

10. While the flag.psd layer is selected, go to Layer➡Pre-compose.

11. Name it flag PC, make sure Move all attributes into the new composition is selected, and click OK.

Pre-compose

New composition name: flag PC

○ Leave all attributes in 'Flag'
Use this option to create a new intermediate composition with only 'FLA flag.psd' in it. The new composition will become the source to the current layer.

● Move all attributes into the new composition
Use this option to place the currently selected layers together into a new intermediate composition.

[OK]   [Cancel]

In order to get a clearer understanding of how and why this effect works, you'll make a minor error first to see how it *doesn't* work. Hey, hey, I know! I hate books that lead you through 10 steps and then say, "See, that didn't work, did it?" But trust me, you'll fix your error with one simple mouse click later on. No going back. Who's got that much free time anyway?

12. Make sure your flag PC layer is selected and go to Effect➡Distort➡ Displacement Map.

File Edit Composition Layer **Effect** View Window Help

Last Effect	Shift+Alt+Ctrl+E
Remove All	Shift+Ctrl+E
Save Favorite...	
Apply Favorite...	
Recent Favorites	▶

3D Channel	▶		
Adjust	▶		
Audio	▶		
Blur & Sharpen	▶		
Channel	▶		
Cineon Tools	▶		
Distort	▶	Bezier Warp	
Image Control	▶	Bulge	
Keying	▶	Corner Pin	
Matte Tools	▶	Displacement Map	
Perspective	▶	Mesh Warp	
Render	▶	Mirror	
Simulation	▶	Offset	
Stylize	▶	Polar Coordinates	
Text	▶	PS+ Pinch...	
Time	▶	PS+ Ripple...	
Transition	▶	PS+ Spherize...	
Video	▶	PS+ Twirl...	
		PS+ Wave...	
		PS+ ZigZag...	
		Reshape	
		Ripple	
		Smear	
		Spherize	
		Twirl	
		Wave Warp	

215

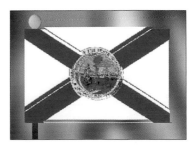

216

13. Change the Displacement Map Layer to Flag Displace.mov.

14. Make a RAM preview and check the motion of your flag.

If your RAM preview looks the way you want it to, move on to the next steps. If not, go back and tweak some of your parameter settings in the Effect Controls window. Now would be a good time to save your project.

The flag is waving like it's floating on water. This is *not* what you want. You need to constrain the displacement effect on the left side, where the flag will be attached to the pole. You can do this by masking off the displacement layer where the flag is supposed to be still.

15. Double-click the Flag Displace.mov layer to open its Layer window.

16. Select the rectangular masking tool from the toolbox.

17. Draw a mask that's slightly indented on the left and goes beyond the layer on the right. It will be easier to make this mask if you first drag and resize this window, giving you ample room to work.

18. You don't want the flag to have a sharp edge where the displacement stops, so you need to feather your mask. Go to Layer➡Mask➡Mask Feather.

19. In the Mask Feather dialog box, uncheck the Lock check box, set Horizontal to 15, and click OK. Then, close the Layer window.

20. Make another RAM preview.

Still not right? That's because you need to add the mask to the video that's being used to displace the flag image. The effect is not taking the mask into account and that is why you will need to pre-compose.

---

21. With the Flag Displace.mov layer selected, pre-compose. Name it displace PC and make sure Move all attributes is selected.

22. Now here's where you can fix your effect with one click. In the Effect Controls window, change flag PC's Displacement Map Layer to displace PC.

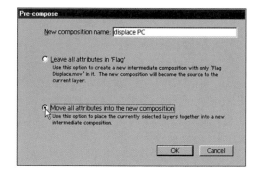

23. Make your final RAM preview.

Yay! Now your flag is waving freely on the right and pinned nicely in place on the left, just the way you wanted. Now would be a good time to Save.

---

24. Duplicate this arrangement of the flag and flagpole elements in the main comp window.

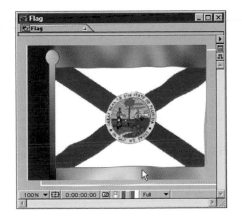

25. You left the displace layer's visibility on in order to adjust your mask placement and to see how the masking affects the flag image. Now that you're happy with the way the flag waves, go ahead and turn it off. Toggle off the displace PC video switch (eye icon) at the far left of the Time Layout Window.

It's time to render your final movie with all the correct settings for your appropriate output and/or distribution method. Now would be a good time to save your project.

TIP

You can also do the Make Movie command by pressing Ctrl+M on the PC or Cmd+M on the Mac.

26. With the current Composition or Time Layout window as the active window, or with the Composition's name/icon selected in the Project window, go up to your menu bar and select Composition➡Make Movie.

27. A Save Movie As dialog box opens. Save the movie as Waving flag.

28. The Render Queue opens next. Here you need to change Render Settings from Current Settings to Best Settings.

29. Next, click on the underlined Output Module setting and change the output module to your choice of format. Check "Import into project when done" so you can quickly see your movie once it's finished rendering.

Output Module Settings

Output Module

Format: QuickTime Movie ▾   ☑ Import into project when done

Amiga IFF Sequence
Animated GIF
☑ Video BMP Sequence
Cineon AE Format Sequence
ElectricImage IMAGE
Format C FLC/FLI
Sorenson V Filmstrip   annels: RGB ▾
Spatial Qua JPEG Sequence
JPEG Sequence   Depth: Millions of Colors ▾
PCX Sequence
PICT Sequence   Color: Premultiplied (With Black) ▾
PNG Sequence
☐ Str Photoshop Sequence
Pixar Sequence   ☑ Lock Aspect Ratio to (4:3)
Renderi QuickTime Movie
SGI Sequence   Custom ▾
Stret TIFF Sequence
Stret Targa Sequence   Stretch Quality: High ▾
Video For Windows
☐ Crop
T: 0   L: 0   B: 0   R: 0   Final Size: 320 x 240

☐ Audio Output
Format Options...
44.100 KHz ▾   16 Bit ▾   Stereo ▾

OK   Cancel

30. In the same Output Module Settings dialog box, click on the Format Options button in the Video Output section.

Output Module Settings

Output Module

Format: QuickTime Movie ▾   ☑ Import into project when done

☑ Video Output

Format Options...
Sorenson Video Compressor   Channels: RGB ▾
Spatial Quality = Most (100)
Depth: Millions of Colors ▾
Color: Premultiplied (With Black) ▾

☐ Stretch
Width   Height
Rendering at: 320   x   240   ☑ Lock Aspect Ratio to (4:3)
Stretch to: 320   x 240   Custom ▾
Stretch %:   x   Stretch Quality: High ▾

☐ Crop
T: 0   L: 0   B: 0   R: 0   Final Size: 320 x 240

NOTE

In this particular project you are choosing the Animation codec to save your final tutorial movie because I tried using the Sorenson codec and it made the movie look so ugly I couldn't live with the compression. I affectionately call this process the "Compression Threshold of Pain."

31. The Compression Settings dialog box pops up. For this example, choose Animation for your compressor and set it to Best quality. Click OK when done.

TIP

If you checked the "Import into project when done" checkbox in the Output Module, simply double-click on the movie icon in your Project window.

TIP

If you plan on sharing your project file with others, especially cross-platform, you need to add the .aep extension to your project name.

32. When the Render Queue is finally ready, click Render.

After the render is complete, play your movie to make sure it came out the way you expected. If all is well, save your final project as Flag.

Part VI

Particle Playground Effects

The raw artwork supplied for this chapter was created using Adobe Illustrator and Adobe Photoshop.

CHAPTER
12

Making Blood Drip from Text

This technique uses basic text to show off its simplicity, but any graphic or video file could be substituted for an even better effect. This technique is commonly used in commercials.

Don't be put off by the gory title—the effect you'll learn in this chapter is worth it. This effect is useful for making objects drop or drip from another object. For example, you could make coins drop from a piggy bank, dollar signs fall from a business chart, or blood drip from text.

1. Open a new project by clicking File➡New➡New Project.

File | Edit | Composition | Layer | Effect | View | Window | Help
New   ▶   New Project   ⌘⌥N
Open...   ⌘O   New Folder   ⌘⇧⌥N

Close   ⌘W
Save   ⌘S
Save As...
Save a Copy...
Revert

Import   ▶
Export   ▶

Add Footage to Comp   ⌘/
Consolidate All Footage
Remove Unused Footage
Collect Files...
Watch Folder...

Set Proxy   ▶
Interpret Footage   ▶
Replace Footage   ▶
Reload Footage   ⌘⌥L

Preferences   ▶
Templates   ▶

Recent Footage   ▶
Recent Projects   ▶

Adobe Online...

Quit   ⌘Q

2. Create a new composition by choosing Composition➡New Composition.

File | Edit | Composition | Layer | Effect | View | Window | Help
New Composition...   ⌘N

Composition Settings...   ⌘K
Background Color...   ⌘⇧B
Set Poster Time

Add To Render Queue   ⌘⇧/
Add Output Module

Preview   ▶
Save Frame As   ▶
Make Movie...   ⌘M
Save RAM Preview...

Comp Flowchart View

227

TIP

You can also create a
new composition by
pressing Ctrl+N on the
PC or Cmd+N on the
Mac.

3. In the Composition Settings dialog box, animate your text in a 320×240 composition window because this will be the size of your finished movie. You're going to work at 15 frames per second, with a duration of 5 seconds. Name it Drip. Click OK when you're done.

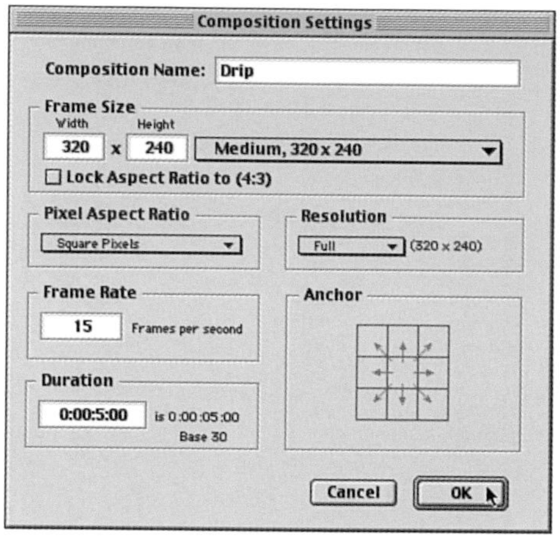

4. To add the image you'll be using as a background, choose File➡Import➡Footage File.

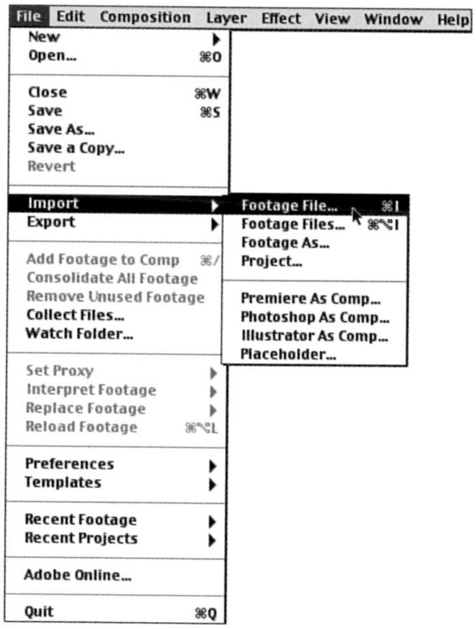

5. Select Haunted.jpg in the Artwork folder for this chapter.

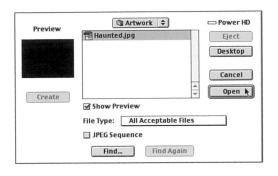

Now that you've imported the graphic file that you plan to use for this project, it's time to move it from the Project window to the Time Layout window. You'll also add some text and effects to this project. Now would be a good time to save your project.

6. Drag Haunted.jpg from the Project window to the Time Layout window.

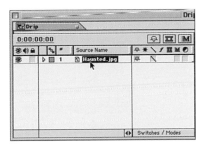

7. The rest of the project materials will be created directly in After Effects. Create a new solid by choosing Layer→New Solid.

TIP

You can also import footage by doing the following:

PC—Right-click in the project window, or press Ctrl+I.

Mac—Hold down the Ctrl key and click in the project window, or press Cmd+I.

Or you can simply double-click inside the Project window in the white area (*not* on a file).

TIP

As a general rule, it's always a good idea to save your project periodically throughout the creative process. This will save you many headaches in the long run. It's also a good idea to save your project with different names throughout the process (project a, project b, project c, etc.). This way you can go back a few steps if you see that your experimentation has taken you in a different direction than where you want to end up.

8. Name your new solid layer Text. Make sure the layer is the same size as your composition (320×240) and click OK.

Solid Settings

Name: Text

Size: Width 320 Height 240 Units pixels

100.0% 100.0%
of composition size [Comp Size]

☐ Lock Aspect Ratio to (4:3)

Color: [   ] ✎

[Cancel] [OK]

9. With the Text layer still selected, go to Effect➡Text➡Basic Text.

| File | Edit | Composition | Layer | **Effect** | View | Window | Help |

Brightness & Contrast ⌘⇧⌥E
Remove All ⌘⇧E

Save Favorite...
Apply Favorite...
Recent Favorites ▸

Adjust ▸
Audio ▸
Blur & Sharpen ▸
Channel ▸
Cineon Tools ▸
Distort ▸
Evolution ▸
Image Control ▸
Keying ▸
Perspective ▸
Render ▸
Stylize ▸
Text ▸ | Basic Text
Time ▸ | Numbers
Transition ▸ | Path Text
Video ▸

10. In the text window, you choose your font, style, direction, and alignment, and then you enter your text. Type in Happy Halloween, accept the default settings, and click OK. You'll notice that the text layer automatically changes from a solid color to your Happy Halloween text.

Font: Arial
Style: Regular

Direction:
● Horizontal
○ Vertical
☐ Rotate

Alignment: ○ Left
● Center
○ Right

Happy Halloween

☑ Show Font [Cancel] [OK]

230

11. In the Effects Control window, click on Fill Color and choose a nice red.

12. Your text is now red, and it's located in the middle of the Composition window.

13. Move your new Text layer to the top of the Composition window, above the haunted house.

In steps 14–18 you'll create the shapes of your drops of blood. You will accomplish this by using the Pen tool to draw the shape on a new Solid layer.

14. First, make another new solid and name it Drop (see steps 7 and 8). This time you want to change the solid's color to match your text, so use the eyedropper to pick the color from Happy Halloween. Click OK.

TIP
You can also open the Layer window by double-clicking on the layer's name in the Time Layout window or by double-clicking on the layer in the Composition window.

232

15. Here's where your drawing skills come into play. You want to mask this new solid into the shape of a drop of liquid. Open this layer into a new window by choosing Layer➡Open Layer Window.

16. The drop will be small compared to the main comp, so zoom in three times to about 800% by pressing the period key on your keyboard. Use the Pen tool to draw a mask in the shape of a drop of liquid.

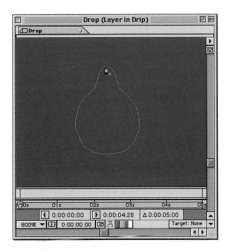

TIP

Pressing the period zooms in the Comp or Layer window, allowing you to see a tight view of the object. To zoom out and return to normal, press the comma.

The zoom amount is reflected in the magnification ratio pop-up in the bottom-left corner of the Comp and Layer windows.

17. After the initial shape is completed, you can go back and smooth it to your liking using the Selection tool.

TIP

Select any point on the mask and the Beziér control points will appear. You can drag, rotate, and move these points as desired to get exactly the shape you want.

233

18. The end points must connect for this effect to work, so go to Layer➡Mask➡ Closed. If you have a checkmark next to Closed, you've already connected your end points. Close the layer window when you're finished.

Now you're going to use this drop shape as a Layer Map in Particle Playground. However, if you leave it as-is, the mask won't hold. First you have to pre-compose this layer.

19. With the Drop layer selected in the Time Layout window, choose Layer➡Pre-compose.

20. Change the name to Drop PC so you know it's a pre-composed layer and not the original. Select Move all attributes into the new composition and click OK.

TIP
A quick way to pre-compose a layer is to select it and press Ctrl+Shift+C on the PC or Cmd+Shift+C on the Mac.

> **Pre-compose**
>
> New composition name: Drop PC
>
> ○ **Leave all attributes in "Drip"**
> Use this option to create a new intermediate composition with only "Drop" in it. The new composition will become the source to the current layer.
>
> ● **Move all attributes into the new composition**
> Use this option to place the currently selected layers together into a new intermediate composition.
>
> Cancel   OK

21. You won't actually view the Drop PC layer in your final composition, so turn off its visibility by clicking the eye in the Time Layout window.

> **Drip**
>
> 0:00:00:00
>
> | | # | Source Name |
> |---|---|---|
> | ▷ | 1 | Drop PC |
> | ▷ | 2 | Text |
> | ▷ | 3 | Haunted.jpg |
>
> Switches / Modes

235

22. Now it's time to create your major effects layer. As before, create a new solid. Name it Particles.

> **Solid Settings**
>
> Name: Particles
>
> | | Width | Height | Units |
> |---|---|---|---|
> | Size: | 320 | 240 | pixels |
>
> 100.0%   100.0%
> of composition size   Comp Size
>
> ☐ Lock Aspect Ratio to (4:3)
>
> Color: ▢
>
> Cancel   OK

23. Select Effect➡Simulation➡Particle Playground.

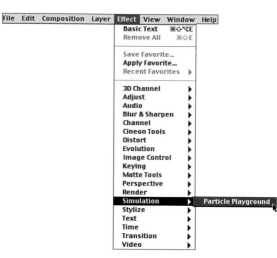

Wow, there's a lot to play with here (which explains the name). For this project, let's keep it simple and do it one step at a time. However, if you feel you must, you can turn to Chapter 4 in the Adobe After Effects Production Bundle User Guide to get more information than you really want.

---

24. First, click on the triangle to the left of Cannon to reveal its list of controls.

25. Click the crosshair next to Position and place it over the H in Happy just outside of the main Composition window.

26. Change the numeric values of the following controls by clicking on them:

- Barrel Radius to about 10.
- Particles Per Second to 4.
- Direction to 180 degrees.
- Direction Random Spread to 0.
- Velocity to around 60.
- Velocity Random Spread to 2.

237

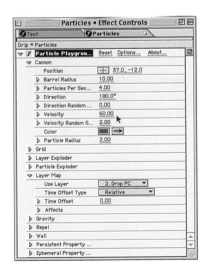

RAM previews are meant to show portions of the composition rather than the entire thing, and how much you'll see depends on how much free RAM you have. For this reason, be sure to temporarily adjust your composition's Work Area Markers before creating a RAM preview. The quickest method is to set the Current Time marker at the desired beginning frame, press the hotkey B, move the marker to the desired ending frame, and press the hotkey N.

With the start point and end point set for the Work Area, there are two methods for creating a RAM preview. You can go to Window, Show Time Controls (or press Ctrl+3 on the PC or Cmd+3 on the Mac) and click the arrow button on the far-right side of the Time Controls box. Or, you can press 0 on your keyboard's numeric keypad.

27. Click open the Layer Map and set Use Layer to Drop PC.

If you hold down the Shift key while making a RAM preview, After Effects will only cache *every other frame*. This trick can be a huge timesaver, especially if the only reason you're making a RAM preview is to check the basic motion of your layers.

Now make a RAM preview and check your work so far. If it looks the way you want it to, move on to the next steps. If not, go back and tweak some of your parameter settings in the Effect Controls window. Now would be a good time to save your project.

When you're ready to move on, the next step is to add some blurriness to the drops to improve the motion effect.

28. Make sure your Particles layer is still selected in the Time Layout window, and then choose Effect➡Blur & Sharpen➡Fast Blur.

29. Set Blurriness to 7 and Blur Dimensions to Vertical.

30. Create another dripping layer by first selecting Particles in the Time Layout window and then choosing Edit➡Duplicate.

31. With the duplicate Particles layer highlighted in the Time Layout window, press the Enter key (Return on the Mac) and type in the name Particles 2. Press Enter/Return again to enter the name change.

239

32. Open this layer's effects by selecting Layer➡Open Effect Controls. Any and all effects will be selected by default, so you need to make sure only Particle Playground is selected before continuing.

33. Click the crosshair next to Position, and then place the Position Cannon over the H in Halloween just outside of the main Composition window.

34. To keep the drops from appearing too similar, adjust Particles Per Second to 6 and Velocity to 75.

35. Move both Particles layers below the text layer in the Time Layout window.

Make another RAM preview. The drips look odd because they appear onscreen fully formed. It would be better if they faded in somehow, but there's no fade option with Particle Playground. Never fear—After Effects has the solution you need.

36. Make sure you are at Time Marker 0:00 and create another New Solid by choosing Layer➡New Solid. Name it ramp1. Accept the defaults and click OK.

NOTE

You're creating a gradient layer that will be revealed through the particles layer. This gradient layer will become the matte that will allow you to create your drips. The appearance and positioning of the gradient will determine where and how your drips will fade in and fall.

241

37. Go to Effect➡Render➡Ramp.

38. You need to adjust the start and end of the ramp so that the gradient is sharper and placed near the bottom of both of the letters H. To begin this process, move ramp1 below the bottom Particles layer in the layer stack in the Time Layout window.

39. Locate the start point at the top center of the Composition window.

40. Click and drag on the start point while holding down the Shift key on your keyboard. Drag the start point to the middle of the text.

41. Locate the end point at the bottom center of the Composition window.

42. Click and drag on the end point while holding down the Shift key on your keyboard. Drag the end point to bottom of the text.

TIP

Pressing the Shift key while you drag ensures that you move the end point in a straight line (in this case, vertically). This will make your gradient even.

243

43. Change the end color to that of the text by using the eyedropper. This will make your drops the same red as everything else.

44. In the Time Layout window, toggle Switches/Modes to Modes.

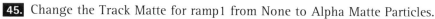

45. Change the Track Matte for ramp1 from None to Alpha Matte Particles.

46. In the Effect Controls window, change the start color to that of the dark gray part of the sky by using the eyedropper tool. This will make your drops look like they're appearing from out of nowhere.

47. Duplicate ramp1. Rename this layer ramp2 and place it just below the Particles2 layers.

48. Change the Track Matte for ramp2 from None to Alpha Matte Particles2.

[Drip • Time Layout window screenshot]

TIP

If you duplicated ramp1 correctly, this may have already been done for you. However, you may need to turn off the video for the Particles 2 layer.

49. Your Time Layout window should now look like the following figure.

[Drip • Time Layout window screenshot]

245

Now make a RAM preview and check the motion of your drip. If it looks the way you want it to, move on to the next steps. If not, go back and tweak some of your settings.

If you're happy with your project after looking at the RAM preview, it's time to render your final movie with all the correct settings for your appropriate output and/or distribution method. Now would be a good time to save your project.

50. With the current Composition or Time Layout window as the active window, or with the Composition's name/icon selected in the Project window, go up to your menu bar and select Composition➡Make Movie.

[Menu screenshot showing Composition menu with options: New Composition... ⌘N, Composition Settings... ⌘K, Background Color... ⌘⇧B, Set Poster Time, Add To Render Queue ⌘⇧/, Add Output Module, Preview ▶, Save Frame As ▶, Make Movie... ⌘M, Save RAM Preview..., Comp Flowchart View]

TIP

You can also do the Make Movie command by pressing Ctrl+M on the PC or Cmd+M on the Mac.

51. A Save Movie As dialog box opens. Save the movie to your desired folder or directory as Drip.mov.

52. The Render Queue will open next. Here you need to change Render Settings from Current Settings to Best Settings.

53. Next, click on the underlined Output Module setting and change the output module to your choice of format (QuickTime Movie was used in this example). Check Import into project when done so you can quickly see your movie once it's finished rendering.

54. In the same Output Module Settings dialog box, click on the Format Options button in the Video Output section.

55. The Compression Settings dialog box pops up. For this example, choose Animation for your compressor and set it to Best quality. Click OK twice to get back to the Render Queue.

247

TIP

If you checked the Import into project when done check box in the Output Module, simply double-click on the movie icon in your Project window.

TIP

If you plan to share your project file with others, especially cross-platform, you need to add the .aep extension to your project name.

56. When the Render Queue is finally ready, click Render.

After the render is complete, play your movie to make sure it came out the way you expected. If all is well, save your final project as Blood Drip.

Part VII

Motion Math Effects

*The logo supplied for this chapter was created using Adobe Illustrator. The background animations come from the Digital Juice: JumpBacks collection (**http:www.digitaljuice.com**). You'll need the Production Bundle of After Effects to complete this chapter.*

CHAPTER 13

Down and Dirty Dynamic Logo Creation Using Audio

This technique can be used on most any image with an alpha channel. Creating animation from an audio file makes it all the more dynamic. You see it used for openings, promos, bumpers, corporate IDs, and animated logos of all types.

At some point in your motion graphics career, a client is going to come to you with a logo that's so plain or so ugly that you'll immediately offer to create a whole new logo for him. Unfortunately, the president of the company will be very attached to the logo (probably because he created it himself), so the marketing manager will ask you to create a new corporate identity using the existing artwork. Naturally, they'll want to use this new piece as the opening to all their videotapes, CD-ROMs, and sales presentations, so it will have to be extra-colorful and dynamic, "like you see on TV." Of course, they'll only have a little bit of money, but they'll promise to give you all their graphics and video work in the future...

This chapter shows you a quick and easy way to create great-looking motion graphics from plain black and white artwork. You'll use stock video/animation, layers and transfer modes, and the AE Motion Math plug-in applied to a sound file to create a very dynamic animation in minutes.

The fictional company you'll be working for in this chapter is Digital Video Consultants. They're a highly qualified group of engineers who network broadcast video systems but don't have a single creative bone in their bodies. Their logo is a simple Adobe Illustrator file made up of a circle, three letters (DVC), and their corporate name "in the round."

1. Open a new project by selecting File➡New➡New Project.

2. Import the Illustrator file and all of the graphic layers associated with it by choosing File➡Import➡Illustrator As Comp.

251

3. Navigate to the Artwork folder for this chapter and select DVC.ai. Click Open.

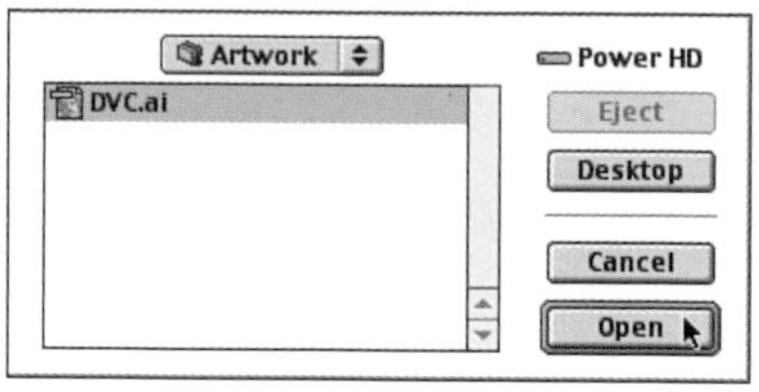

TIP

You can also import multiple footage files by pressing Ctrl+Alt+I on the PC or Cmd+Option +I on the Mac.

4. To add the stock animation files you'll be working with in this chapter, choose File➡Import➡Footage Files.

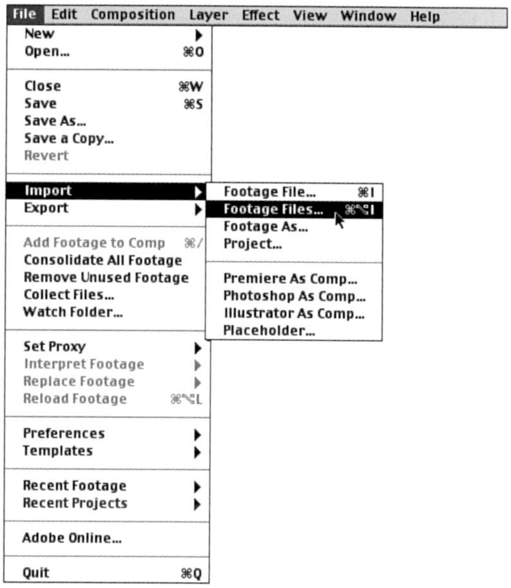

252

5. The Import dialog box should open back up to the Artwork folder for this chapter. Select jb_001.mov and click Open.

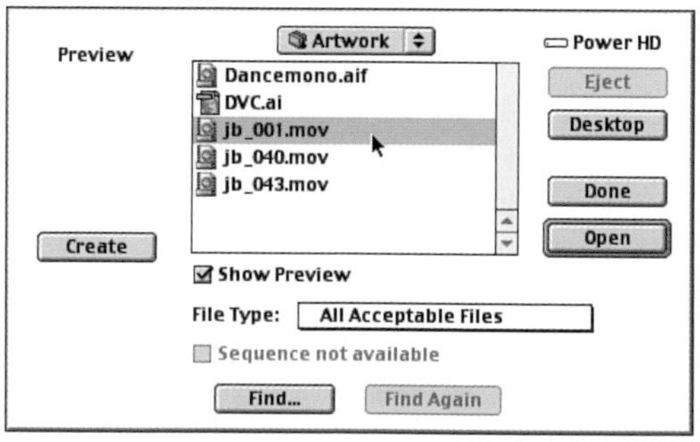

6. The Import dialog box will remain open. This time, select jb_040.mov. Click Open.

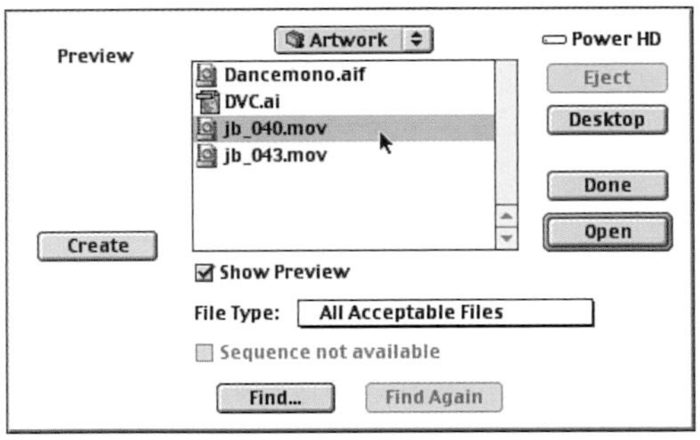

7. With the Import dialog box still open, select jb_043.mov and click Open.

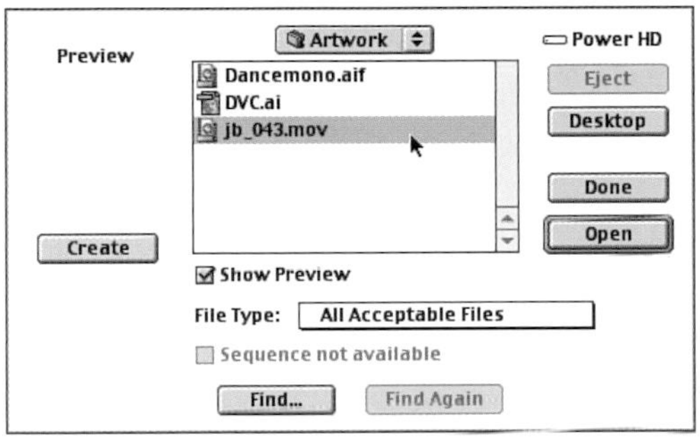

253

NOTE

Even though the files jb_001.mov, jb_040.mov, and jb_043.mov are only 320×240 pixels in size (for use with this chapter), they're also provided as full-size, broadcast-quality, royalty-free clips on the Goodies CD included with this book.

8. Last but not least, choose the audio file you'll incorporate into your project by selecting Dancemono.aif. Click Open, and then click Done.

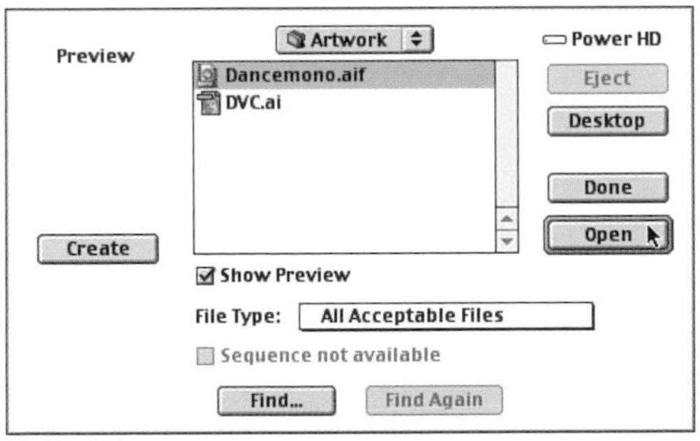

NOTE

The items in the folder are the individual layers within the Illustrator file.

9. You now have a number of items in your Project window, including a folder and a composition that are both named DVC.ai. Click on the triangle next to the folder named DVC.ai. It now displays the contents of the folder.

TIP

As a general rule, it's always a good idea to save your project periodically throughout the creative process. This will save you many headaches in the long run. It's also a good idea to save your project with different names throughout the process (project a, project b, project c, etc.). This way you can go back a few steps if you see that your experimentation has taken you in a different direction than where you want to end up.

The imported Illustrator file, with both of its layers, is the first item you'll work with in the After Effects Time Layout window. You'll be adding motion, assigning Transfer Modes, and creating alpha mattes to bring this project to life. Now would be a good time to save your project.

10. Double-click on the DVC.ai Composition. This will open the Time Layout window and the Composition window.

NOTE

The size of the composition is taken from the size of the original Illustrator file (determined by the size of the artwork, or by the cropmarks).

TIP

You can also open the Composition Settings window by pressing Cmd+K on the Mac or Ctrl+K on the PC.

11. All of the Illustrator layers now appear as composition layers in the After Effects Time Layout window in their correct order.

12. Unfortunately, you can't count on After Effects to keep everything correct. Although it kept the size correct at 320×240, it will set the frame rate and duration to what you used last. To be on the safe side, go to Composition➡Composition Settings and set Frame Rate to 15 and Duration to 8 seconds. Click OK when you're done.

```
Composition Settings

Composition Name: DVC.ai

┌ Frame Size ──────────────────────────────┐
│   Width      Height                        │
│   320  x   240    Medium, 320 x 240   ▼   │
│  ☐ Lock Aspect Ratio to (4:3)              │
└───────────────────────────────────────────┘

┌ Pixel Aspect Ratio ──┐  ┌ Resolution ──────────┐
│  Square Pixels    ▼  │  │  Full   ▼  (320 x 240)│
└──────────────────────┘  └───────────────────────┘

┌ Frame Rate ──────────┐  ┌ Anchor ──────────────┐
│  15   Frames per second│  │                      │
└──────────────────────┘  │                      │
                          │                      │
┌ Duration ────────────┐  │                      │
│  0:00:08:00  is 0:00:08:00│                    │
│              Base 30   │  └──────────────────────┘
└──────────────────────┘

                        Cancel      OK
```

13. Because the black logo is sitting on a black background, you cannot see the DVC logo at this time. To remedy this, drag the jb_001.mov clip from the Project window to the Time Layout window. Make sure that the Current Time Marker is at 0:00.

```
DVC.ai • Time Layout

DVC.ai
0:00:00:00
         # │ Layer Name              :00s   02s   04s   06s   08s
    ▷ □ 1  │ [jb_001.mov]
    ▷ □ 2  │ Text
    ▷ □ 3  │ DVC Logo

              Switches / Modes
```

14. Move the jb_001.mov clip from the top of the Time Layout window to the bottom of the layer stack in the Time Layout window.

```
DVC.ai • Time Lay

DVC.ai
0:00:00:00
         # │ Layer Name
    ▷ □ 1  │ Text
    ▷ □ 2  │ DVC Logo
    ▷ □ 3  │ [jb_001.mov]

              Switches / Modes
```

NOTE

You may need to adjust your layer durations after you change your composition duration. If your layers are to short (don't extend to the end of your timeline) simply drag their endpoint to the end of your Time Layout window.

TIP

To make Adobe Illustrator files import into Adobe After Effects at a specific size, you need to set crop marks in the Illustrator file:

1. Select the Rectangle tool and click once on your document.

2. A dialog box will open. Enter your dimensions (width and height). Click OK.

3. With the Rectangle tool still selected, go to Objects➡Crop Marks.

If you don't want to be this specific, use the Rectangle tool to draw a rectangle around your Illustrator object. Then, set your Stroke and Fill to none (so you don't end up with a black/colored square/outline over your image). Lastly, position your rectangle where you want your cropped edges to be.

255

TIP

You can also simply click and drag down the layer stack over each of the layers' Quality switches to change them all as you go.

15. The last thing you need to do before you begin animating your layers is change each layer's Quality level from Draft to Best. You can do this by clicking once on each of the dotted backslash lines to turn them into solid forward-slash lines.

TIP

You might want to take a look at the individual layers of your composition before you start animating them. This would give you a good idea of the elements that you are about to work with.

The easiest way to do this is to turn on and off the layers' video switches to look at each one.

256

Now that you have the basic elements in place, it's time to begin the animation process. First, you'll rotate the text so that it spins around the outside of the logo. Then, you'll fill the black portion of the logo with a moving texture. Now would be a good time to save your project.

16. Select the Text layer (layer 1).

17. Press the letter R on your keyboard to reveal the Rotation Property for this layer.

18. Click once on the Rotation stopwatch icon.

19. Press the letter O on your keyboard to go to the Out point for this layer.

257

20. Click once on underlined 0.0° to bring up the Rotation dialog box.

NOTE
You have now set the circular text (layer 1) to rotate 180° over the length of your composition.

21. Type in 180 under Degrees and click the OK button.

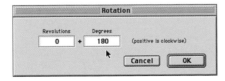

The DVC logo layer now acts as an alpha matte through which the video of layer 3 "jb_001.mov" is revealed. Notice that the video switch for the DVC Logo layer has been turned off automatically as only it's alpha channel information is being used.

Track Matte sets up a matte and fill relationship between two layers positioned one on top of the other in the layer stack. After it is enabled, the Track Matte allows the bottom layer to show through areas of the top layer based on the top layer's alpha or luminance values.

An Alpha matte allows the bottom layer to show through areas of the top layer that have alpha channel pixel values of greater than 0%. Areas that have alpha channel pixel values of 100% will appear completely opaque, and those with values between 1% and 99% appear semitransparent.

A Luma matte allows the bottom layer to show through areas of the top layer that have luminance values of greater than 0%. Areas that have luminance values of 100% will appear completely opaque, and those with values between 1% and 99% appear semitransparent.

22. Now click once on the Switches/Modes button at the bottom of your Time Layout window to change the view to Modes.

23. For layer 3, change the Track Matte from No Track Matte to Alpha Matte "DVC Logo". This will fill the black portions of your logo with the animated background.

24. Make a RAM preview.

You'll notice that the logo filled with the jb_001.mov file provides a very nice animated texture that required no extra work on your part to create. You'll now build a multilayered animated background for your logo to play on.

25. Make sure your Time Marker is at the 0:00-.

258

26. Drag the jb_040.mov clip from the Project window to the Time Layout window, and move it to the bottom so that it's now layer 4.

27. Notice how the jb_040.mov clip is only 2 seconds in length. To make it fit the length of your project, you'll need to make it loopable.

28. With the jb_040.mov clip still selected in the Project window, go to File➡Interpret Footage➡Main.

259

29. At the bottom of the Interpret Footage dialog box, set Looping to 4. Click OK when you're done.

The Out point of the layer duration bar does not automatically lengthen to reflect the looped length. However, the outline of the layer duration bar is longer indicating that there is more of this layer available.

260

30. Back in the Time Layout window, drag the Out point (tail end) of your jb_040.mov clip to the end of your timeline. You now have a seamlessly looped background animation!

Your looped background animation is okay, but you can make it a lot more colorful and dynamic by adding Transfer Modes and an additional clip. Now would be a good time to save your project.

You can also duplicate an item by pressing Cmd+D on the Mac or Ctrl+D on the PC.

31. With Layer 4 still selected, go to the Edit menu and choose Duplicate.

32. You should now have two copies of the jb_040.mov clip in your Time Layout window.

33. Make sure your Time Marker is set to 0, and then drag the jb_043.mov clip from the Project window to the Time Layout window. Move it to the bottom of the layer stack so that it is now layer 6.

261

34. On layer 4, change the Transfer Mode from Normal to Soft Light.

TIP

The use of the Soft Light and Screen Transfer Modes allow you to quickly and easily add various degrees of transparency to your layers.

35. On layer 5, change the Transfer Mode from Normal to Screen.

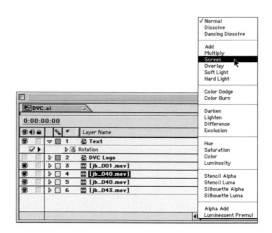

Make a RAM preview and you'll see that in just a few steps, you've created a very colorful flowing background from existing footage. Now you'll add the finishing touches by placing an audio file in your composition and automatically animating your logo to the beat of the music. You'll need the Production Bundle of After Effects to complete this part.

36. Make sure your Time Marker is set to 0, and then drag the Dancemono.aif clip from the Project window to the Time Layout window. Move it to the bottom of the layer stack so that it's now layer 7.

NOTE

Remember that this is the alpha matte through which your logo is being revealed.

37. Select the DVC Logo (layer 2) in the Time Layout window.

38. Choose Layer➡Keyframe Assistant➡Motion Math.

```
File  Edit  Composition  Layer  Effect  View  Window  Help
                         New Solid...                    ⌘Y
                         New Adjustment Layer
                         Solid Settings...               ⌘⇧Y

                         Open Effect Controls            ⌘⇧T
                         Open Layer Window

                         Mask                      ▶
                         Quality                   ▶
                         Switches                  ▶
                         Transform                 ▶
                         Add Marker

                         Preserve Transparency
                         Transfer Mode             ▶
                         Track Matte               ▶

                         Bring Layer to Front      ⌘⇧]
                         Bring Layer Forward       ⌘]
                         Send Layer Backward       ⌘[
                         Send Layer to Back        ⌘⇧[

                         Toggle Hold Keyframe      ⌘⌥H
                         Keyframe Interpolation... ⌘⌥K
                         Keyframe Velocity...      ⌘⇧K
                         Keyframe Assistant        ▶     Easy Ease
                                                         Easy Ease In
                         Enable Time Remapping     ⌘⌥T   Easy Ease Out
                         Time Stretch...                 Exponential Scale
                         Pre-compose...            ⌘⇧C   Motion Math...
                                                         Motion Stabilizer...
                                                         Motion Tracker...
                                                         Sequence Layers...
                                                         Time-Reverse Keyframes
```

39. The Motion Math dialog box opens. Click the Load button at the bottom of the dialog box.

```
                          Motion Math
Program Text:
// Copy Values - Version 4.0
// This Program Sets the value of the first set of popups to the
// value of the second set of popups multiplied by a scale factor.

//   LAYER                PROPERTY            CHANNEL
//   -----                --------            -------
// 1: layer to copy values to    property copied to    channel of property to copy to
// 2: layer to copy values from  property copied from  channel of property to copy from

scale_factor = 1.0;
value(pop_layer(1), pop_property(1)) [pop_channel(1)] =
  value(pop_layer(2), pop_property(2)) [pop_channel(2)] * scale_factor;

Functions: [▼]  Math Functions: [▼]  Operators: [▼]  Constants: [▼]
   Layer:                    Property:              Channel:
1: [ DVC Logo         ▼]    [ Rotation      ▼]    [ All    ▼]
2: [ Text             ▼]    [ Rotation      ▼]    [ All    ▼]
Errors:
No Errors

◉ Sample at:  [    15    ] Samples per second
○ Sample only at existing keyframes

[ Load...  ]  [ Save... ]        [ Cancel ]  [ Apply ]
```

> **NOTE**
>
> Yikes! This is the scary dialog box that makes most new Motion Math users click on the Cancel button. Don't be afraid of it. The Adobe After Effects Production Bundle ships with several incredibly useful Motion Math scripts that are ready to use. No programming required.
>
> However, if you're a true propeller-head, you can get the most out of this incredible feature by writing your own scripts or modifying those that ship with After Effects.

40. Navigate to the Motion Math Scripts folder located in your After Effects application folder and select the cmpaud.mm file. Click Open.

41. Notice that everything you need to know about how this script operates is located in the script's comments. Basically, the cmpaud script (which stands for Comp Audio) will set the value of the first pop-up menu to the audio level of the comp. That's easy enough!

264

42. Make sure that your DVC Logo layer appears in the #1 Layer pop-up.

43. Make sure your Scale property appears in the #1 Property pop-up.

44. Locate the max = 1000 variable in the script window.

```
                          Motion Math

Program Text:
// Comp Audio Version 1.2

// This Program Sets the value of the first set of popups
// to the audio level of the comp, scaled to lie within the range [min, max]

//    LAYER                          PROPERTY              CHANNEL
//    -----                          --------              -------
// 1 : Layer to copy audio amplitude into    property to vary    channel of property
// 2 : doesn't matter                        doesn't matter      doesn't matter

max = 1000;    // change this to the maximum value
min = 50;      // change this to the minimum value

Functions: [▼]  Math Functions: [▼]  Operators: [▼]  Constants: [▼]
```

45. Change 1000 to 400. This will cause the logo to only scale as high as 400%. Click Apply when you're done.

```
                          Motion Math

Program Text:
// Comp Audio Version 1.2

// This Program Sets the value of the first set of popups
// to the audio level of the comp, scaled to lie within the range [min, max]

//    LAYER                          PROPERTY              CHANNEL
//    -----                          --------              -------
// 1 : Layer to copy audio amplitude into    property to vary    channel of property
// 2 : doesn't matter                        doesn't matter      doesn't matter

max = 400;    // change this to the maximum value
min = 50;     // change this to the minimum value

Functions: [▼]  Math Functions: [▼]  Operators: [▼]  Constants: [▼]
```

NOTE

For this project, you're using a mono audio file. It will constrain the x- and y-scale changes to the file's original proportions.

If your audio file were in stereo, the script would animate the x-scale and the y-scale independently of each other, one to each channel in the audio. This can lead to some very interesting effects!

265

That's it! Make a RAM preview, and you can easily see how the Motion Math plug-in has animated the logo's Scale parameter to the amplitude of the audio. When the sound gets louder, the logo gets bigger!

If you're happy with your project after looking at the RAM preview, it's time to render your final movie with all the correct settings for your appropriate output and/or distribution method.

46. With the current Composition or Time Layout window as the active window, or with the Composition's name/icon selected in the Project window, go up to your menu bar and select Composition➡Make Movie.

```
File  Edit  Composition  Layer  Effect  View  Window  Help
              New Composition...        ⌘N

              Composition Settings...   ⌘K
              Background Color...        ⌘⇧B
              Set Poster Time

              Add To Render Queue        ⌘⇧/
              Add Output Module

              Preview                    ▶
              Save Frame As              ▶
              Make Movie...              ⌘M
              Save RAM Preview...

              Comp Flowchart View
```

TIP

You can also do the Make Movie command by pressing Ctrl+M on the PC or Cmd+M on the Mac.

47. A Save Movie As dialog box opens. Save the movie as DVC to your desired folder or directory.

48. The Render Queue will open next. Here you need to change Render Settings from Current Settings to Best Settings.

49. Next, click on the underlined Output Module setting and change the output module to your choice of format (QuickTime Movie was used in this example). Check "Import into project when done" so you can quickly see your movie when it's finished rendering.

50. In the same Output Module Settings dialog box, click on the Format
Options button in the Video Output section.

51. The Compression Settings dialog box pops up. For this example, choose
Sorenson Video for your compressor and set it to Best Quality. Click OK.

52. This project has an audio track, so click on the Audio Output module
check box and use these settings: 22.050 KHz, 16 Bit, Mono. Click OK
when you're done.

If you checked the "Import into project when done" check box in the Output Module, simply double-click on the movie icon in your Project window.

If you plan on sharing your project file with others, especially cross-platform, you need to add the .aep extension to your project name.

53. When the Render Queue is finally ready, click Render.

After the render is complete, play your movie to make sure it came out the way you expected. If all is well, save your final project as DVC Opening.

Part VIII

Miscellaneous Effects

The raw artwork supplied for this chapter was created using Adobe Photoshop.

CHAPTER 14

Creating an Animated Jigsaw Puzzle

This type of effect is often used in corporate videos to show how all the different divisions of a company work together to achieve the corporate goal. You'll also see a version of this technique used in the openings of television shows to introduce the cast, although usually the edges of each individual piece are faded to transparency.

Have you ever thought of animating several elements so they come together into a recognizable image, like putting the pieces of a jigsaw puzzle together? Did you abandon the idea because you thought you'd have to dissect the image in Photoshop, import each element, meticulously match up their edges in the main After Effects Comp window, and then consider looking for a new career after the fourth time a piece shifted out of alignment?

Fortunately, After Effects allows you to take an image, chop it apart, and animate the individual pieces. And it does so in a few very easy steps, using only two images. Here's how it's done.

1. Open a new project by clicking File➧New➧New Project.

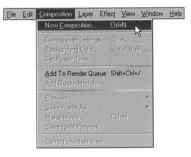

2. Create a new composition by choosing Composition➧New Composition.

274

TIP

You can also create a new composition by pressing Ctrl+N on the PC or Cmd+N on the Mac.

3. In the Composition Settings dialog box, animate your puzzle in a 320×240 composition window because this will be the size of your finished movie. You're going to work at 15 frames per second, with a duration of 10 seconds. Name the composition Polo's Puzzle and click OK.

TIP

You can also import footage by doing the following:

PC—Right-click in the project window, or press Ctrl+I.
Mac—Hold down the Ctrl key and click in the project window, or press Cmd+I.

Or you can simply double-click inside the Project window in the white area (*not* on a file).

4. Now let's bring in your central image. Choose File➡Import➡Footage As.

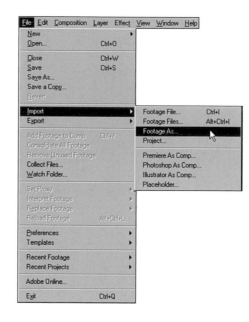

5. Navigate to the Artwork folder for this chapter and select polo's puzzle.jpg. Click Open.

6. Now import puzzle template.jpg, also in the Artwork folder.

275

Now that you've imported the movie file that you plan to use for this project, it's time to move it from the Project window to the Time Layout window. Also, you'll duplicate the layers and begin the colorization process. Now would be a good time to save your project.

7. Drag both items onto the Time Layout window, placing the puzzle template on top.

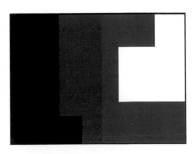

8. Duplicate each of the two layers three times so that you have eight layers stacked as in the following screenshot. (To duplicate a layer, go to Edit➡Duplicate in the menu.)

276

9. Turn off visibility for all but the top two layers by clicking the layer's video switch (eye icon) to the far left of the Time Layout window.

10. Notice how your colored pieces are shaped like "cut-outs" of a puzzle, each with its own assigned color. Turning off the visibility for all but the top two layers will make it easier to see exactly how the puzzle template is being used at this point. In this example, you'll cut the puzzle from left to right, going black, red, blue, and then white. Once you understand this method, you'll find it easy to create your own templates of varying complexity to use in real-world projects.

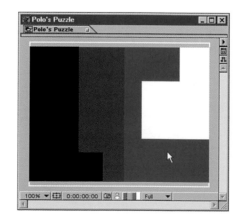

Turning off the visibility for all but the top two layers will make it easier to see exactly how the puzzle template is being used at this point. In steps 12–19, you'll cut the puzzle from left to right, going black, red, blue, and then white. Once you understand this method, you'll find it easy to create your own templates of varying complexity to use in real-world projects.

11. Select the top puzzle template layer (which should be layer 1 at this point), and then go to Effect➡Keying➡Color Key.

12. Choose black for the Key Color control by using the eyedropper over the black portion of the puzzle template.

13. Set Color Tolerance to about 18.

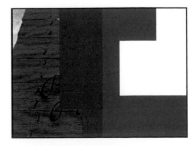

14. Notice how that portion of your template disappears from view in the main Comp window.

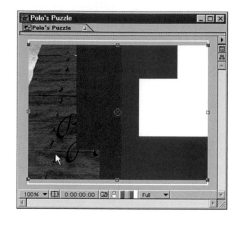

15. At the bottom of the Time Layout window, toggle from Switches to Modes.

16. Change the top polo's puzzle.jpg layer TrkMat (track matte) from No Track Matte to Alpha Inverted Matte "puzzle template.jpg". Notice how the rest of your template has disappeared.

17. Turn on the visibility of the remaining layers (but NOT for layer 1).

18. Copy the Color Key effect and paste it onto the three remaining puzzle template layers.

19. Follow steps 13 and 14 to color key out the remaining colors in your template (red, blue, white).

20. Repeat step 17 for each of the remaining polo's puzzle layers.

TIP

Because you have no effects currently applied to the three remaining puzzle template layers, here's the way to do this:

- Press Ctrl+C on the PC or Cmd+C on the Mac to copy the effect from within the Effect Controls window
- Select one of the remaining puzzle template layers on the Time Layout window
- Press Ctrl+V on the PC or Cmd+V on the Mac to paste the effect here

In the Effect Controls window, a new tab will appear showing the effect applied to the layer. For any additional effects, you can simply copy and paste right in this window without going to the Time Layout window.

279

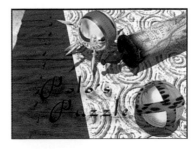

Now you want to pre-compose each pair one by one and name them
Piece1 to Piece4 to help make the animation more manageable. Pre-
composing isn't really necessary, but you'll find that it helps a great
deal as your projects (and puzzles) get more complex. In these complex
situations, grouping layers under a subheading makes keeping track of
all the aspcets of your animated sequence much easier.

21. Highlight the top two layers by selecting layer 1 and then Ctrl+clicking
(or Cmd+clicking on the Mac) on layer 2.

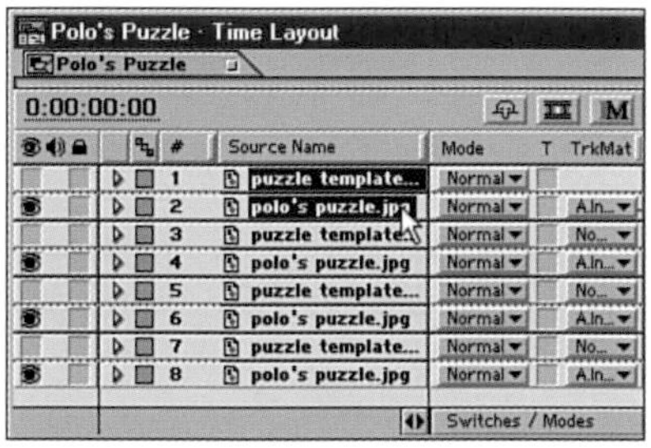

TIP

A quick way to pre-
compose layers is to
select them and then
press Ctrl+Shift+C on
the PC or Cmd+Shift+C
on the Mac.

22. Go to Layer→Pre-compose.

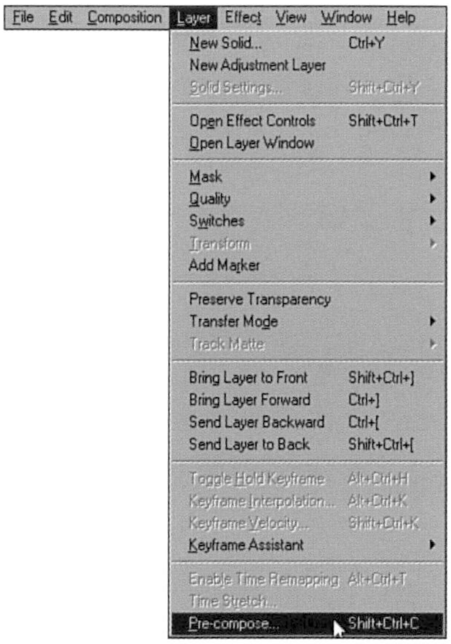

23. Name this first pair Piece1, make sure Move all attributes into the new composition is selected and click OK.

> **Pre-compose**
>
> New composition name: Piece1
>
> ○ Leave all attributes in 'Polo's Puzzle'
> Use this option to create a new intermediate composition with only 'puzzle template.jpg' in it. The new composition will become the source to the current layer.
>
> This option is not available because more than one layer is selected.
>
> ● Move all attributes into the new composition
> Use this option to place the currently selected layers together into a new intermediate composition.
>
> [OK] [Cancel]

24. Repeat steps 22 through 24 for the remaining pairs, naming them sequentially. Your Time Layout window should now look like the following figure.

> **Polo's Puzzle · Time Layout**
> **Polo's Puzzle**
>
> 0:00:00:00
>
> | | | # | Source Name | Mode | T | TrkMat |
> |---|---|---|---|---|---|---|
> | | ▷ ■ | 1 | Piece1 | Normal ▼ | | |
> | | ▷ ■ | 2 | Piece2 | Normal ▼ | | No.. ▼ |
> | | ▷ ■ | 3 | Piece3 | Normal ▼ | | No.. ▼ |
> | | ▷ ■ | 4 | Piece4 | Normal ▼ | | No.. ▼ |
>
> Switches / Modes

NOTE

"Move all attributes into the new composition" is selected by default because we are pre-composing more than one layer.

281

Now it's time to animate your puzzle. Right now all of the edges meet perfectly, so you will reverse-animate by setting keyframes where you want to end and working backwards in time.

TIP

To select all layers, press Ctrl+A on the PC or Cmd+A on the Mac.

25. Select all the layers by going to Edit➡Select All.

> File **Edit** Composition Layer Effect View Window Help
>
> Undo Pre-compose   Ctrl+Z
> Can't Redo   Shift+Ctrl+Z
>
> Cut   Ctrl+X
> Copy   Ctrl+C
> Paste   Ctrl+V
> Clear
>
> Duplicate   Ctrl+D
> Split Layer   Shift+Ctrl+D
> Select All   Ctrl+A
> Deselect All   Shift+Ctrl+A
>
> Label   ▶
>
> Purge   ▶
>
> Edit Original..   Ctrl+E

26. Open each layer's Position property by pressing the hotkey P.

27. On the Time Layout window, move ahead to 8 seconds.

28. Set a keyframe for each layer by clicking on each Position stopwatch icon.

29. Go to the first frame on the Time Layout window.

30. Move each piece in a different direction until the main Comp window is empty. Keep in mind that it's more interesting if pieces cross each other during the animation.

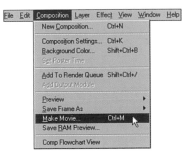

Now make a RAM preview and check the motion of your puzzle pieces. If it looks the way you want it to, move on to the next steps. If not, go back and tweak some of your position settings or keyframes.

If you're happy with your project after looking at the RAM preview, it's time to render your final movie with all the correct settings for your appropriate output and/or distribution method. Now would be a good time to save your project.

31. With the current Composition or Time Layout window as the active window, or with the Composition's name/icon selected in the Project window, go up to your menu bar and select Composition➡Make Movie.

283

NOTE

RAM previews are meant to show portions of the composition rather than the entire thing, and how much you'll see depends on how much free RAM you have. For this reason, be sure to temporarily adjust your composition's Work Area Markers before creating a RAM preview. The quickest method is to set the Current Time marker at the desired beginning frame, press the hotkey B, move the marker to the desired ending frame, and press the hotkey N.

With the Work Area markers set, there are two methods for creating a RAM preview. You can go to Window➡Show Time Controls (or press Ctrl+3 on the PC or Cmd+3 on the Mac) and click the arrow button on the far-right side of the Time Controls box. Or, you can press 0 on your keyboard's numeric keypad.

TIP

If you hold down the Shift key while making a RAM preview, After Effects will only cache *every other frame*. This trick can be a huge timesaver, especially if the only reason you are making a RAM preview is to check the basic motion of your layers.

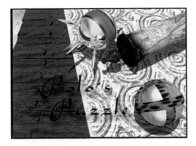

32. A Save Movie As dialog box will open. Save the movie as Polo's Puzzle to your desired folder or directory.

33. The Render Queue will open next. Here you need to change Render Settings from Current Settings to Best Settings.

34. Next, click on the underlined Output Module setting and change the output module to your choice of format. Check "Import into project when done" so you can quickly see your movie once it's finished rendering.

35. In the same Output Module Settings dialog box, click on the Format Options button in the Video Output section.

36. The Compression Settings dialog box pops up. For this example, choose Sorenson Video for your compressor and set it to Best Quality. Click OK when done.

37. When the Render Queue is finally ready, click Render.

After the render is complete, play your movie to make sure it came out the way you expected. If all is well, save your final project as Polo's Puzzle.

285

TIP

If you checked the "Import into project when done" check box in the Output Module, simply double-click on the movie icon in your Project window.

TIP

If you plan on sharing your project file with others, especially cross-platform, you need to add the .aep extension to your project name.

The raw artwork supplied for this chapter was created using Adobe Photoshop and Discreet 3D Studio MAX. You'll need the Production Bundle version of After Effects to complete this tutorial.

CHAPTER
15

Building and Animating an Opening Iris

This technique is used in many sci-fi and space-themed TV shows. It's great for revealing people or products behind a "magical" door. It's also useful for creating a portal that someone can look through or as a window on the side of a spaceship.

Wouldn't it be cool if you could take a flat image, cut it into pieces resembling blades, and then animate it so it opened like a mechanical iris? I thought so too. That's exactly what you're going to do in this project.

Creating 3D-style effects with 2D images is one of the most powerful features of After Effects. It saves rendering time and usually saves some artist time as well. For this project in particular, most of the "hard" steps need to be done only once and then can be copied and pasted to the other layers. This is a very sharp effect made quick and easy.

1. Open a new project by selecting File➡New➡New Project.

2. Create a new composition by choosing Composition➡New Composition.

3. In the Composition Settings dialog box, animate your text in a 320×240 composition window because this will be the size of your finished movie. You're going to work at 15 frames per second, with a duration of three seconds. Name it Iris. Click OK when you're done.

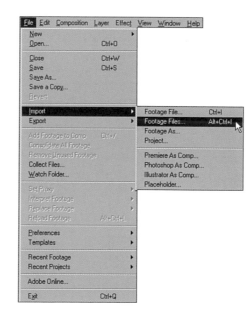

4. Now let's bring in your images. Choose File➡Import➡Footage Files.

5. Select iris colored.tga, iris textured.tga, and star burst.avi in the Artwork folder for this chapter. You can do this by selecting each file and then clicking on the Open button. When you're finished importing, click Done.

In the following steps you will use Color Keys and Matte Tools to key out colored areas and make them transparent. These colored "wedges" is what you will animate later on in the chapter. Now that you've imported the movie and graphic files that you plan to use for this project, it would be a good time to save your project.

6. Drag iris colored.tga and iris textured.tga onto the Time Layout window, placing iris colored.tga on top.

7. Turn off the visibility of iris textured.tga by clicking on the layer's video switch (eye icon) at the far left of the Time Layout window. This will make it easier for you to see exactly how the colored template is being used at this point.

TIP

You can also import multiple footage items by doing the following:

PC—Right-click in the project window or press Alt+Control+I.
Mac—Hold down the Ctrl key and click in the project window, or press Option+Command+I.

TIP

As a general rule, it's always a good idea to save your project periodically throughout the creative process. This will save you many headaches in the long run. It's also a good idea to save your project with different names throughout the process (project a, project b, project c, etc.). This way you can go back a few steps if you see that your experimentation has taken you in a different direction than where you want to end up.

NOTE

If the eye icons are NOT located at the far left of your Time Layout window, then it's because you moved the A/V Features panel. Don't send me email! Just find the icons and go on with your life.

289

8. Select iris colored.tga and go to Effect➡Keying➡Color Key.

290

9. Key out the bright yellow area by clicking on the eyedropper tool and then clicking on the yellow pie wedge.

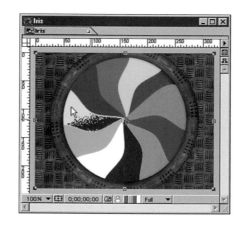

10. Some of the yellow might not key out initially. If this happens, move up Color Tolerance to about 16 while leaving Edge Thin and Edge Feather at zero.

11. Next, go to Effect➡Matte Tools➡Matte Choker.

12. The default settings should be perfect.

13. Now the yellow is gone.

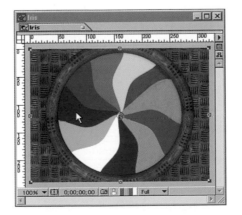

14. Click anywhere on the Time Layout window to make it active, and then duplicate the iris colored.tga layer 10 times (for each of the 10 remaining colored iris sections) by going to Edit➡Duplicate.

15. Shift+select all of the colored iris layers on the Time Layout window.

16. Open the effects for all of these layers by selecting Layer➡Open Effect Controls.

17. One by one, click on each Color Key name to change colors (again using the eyedropper to select the color to be keyed out).

TIP

You might find it easier to select the layer in the Time Layout window first, and then make the change in the Effect Controls window. I also found it easiest to go around the iris in a clockwise direction.

18. Turn on the visibility of iris textured.tga and duplicate it 10 times as well.

293

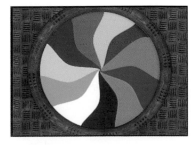

19. Place one copy of iris textured.tga beneath each copy of iris colored.tga so that your Time Layout window looks like the following figure.

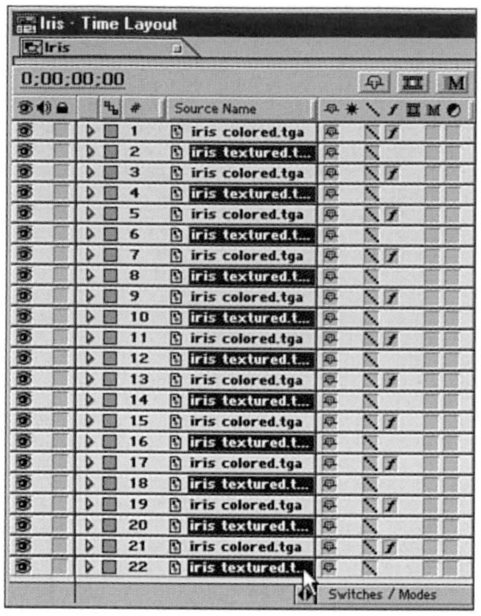

20. At the bottom of the Time Layout window, toggle Switches/Modes to Modes.

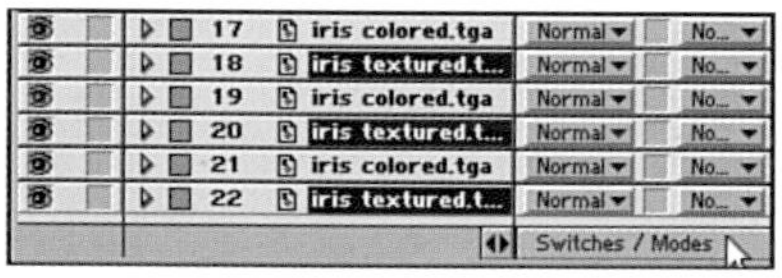

21. Change each iris textured.tga's Track Matte from None to Alpha Inverted Matte "iris colored.tga".

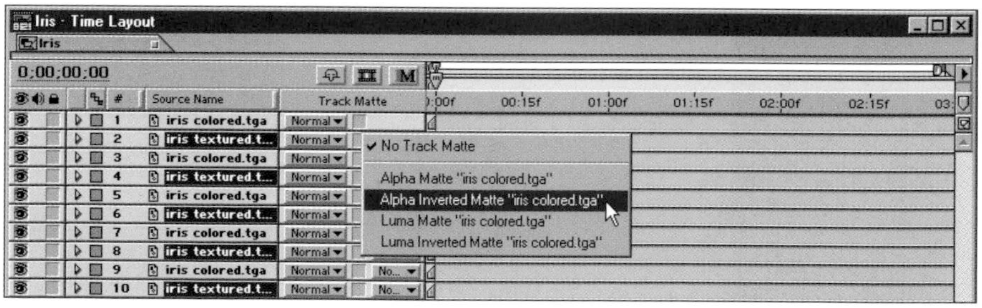

All that you see now are the sections where the colored iris used to be. The next few steps will determine how well the colors are being keyed out. Now would be a good time to save your project.

NOTE

Track Matte sets up a matte and fill relationship between two layers positioned one on top of the other in the layer stack. After it is enabled, the Track Matte allows the bottom layer to show through areas of the top layer based on the top layer's alpha or luminance values.

An Alpha matte allows the bottom layer to show through areas of the top layer that have alpha channel pixel values of greater than 0%. Areas that have alpha channel pixel values of 100% will appear completely opaque, and those with values between 1% and 99% appear semitransparent.

A Luma matte allows the bottom layer to show through areas of the top layer that have luminance values of greater than 0%. Areas that have luminance values of 100% will appear completely opaque, and those with values between 1% and 99% appear semitransparent.

22. Turn off the visibility of all layers.

You can turn off the visibility of all the layers at once. Simply hold down the Alt key on the PC or the Option key on the Mac while clicking on the eye icon of any of the layers.

You can also simply click and drag down the layer stack over each of the layers' Video switches to change them all as you go.

23. Turn on the visibility of textured layer 1 (which is actually layer 2 in the Time Layout window).

24. Check the matte and adjust if necessary. You'll know if your matte needs adjustment if your textured wedge shape in your Composition window doesn't look as clean and clear as you'd like. Items that might need adjustment are Matte Choker and Color Tolerance.

TIP

Do not turn the video on for any of the iris colored.tga layers as this will disrupt the track matte that we have set up for each of the layer pairs.

25. Repeat steps 23 and 24 for the rest of the textured layers.

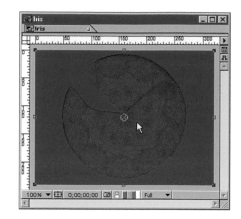

Once all the mattes are clean and crisp, pre-compose all the pairs and name them by color, following this example.

296

26. Select layers 1 and 2.

27. Go to Layer➡Pre-compose.

28. Name the layer according to the color (yellow in this example).

29. Make sure Move all attributes into the new composition is selected, and then click OK.

NOTE

"Move all attributes into the new composition" is selected by default because we are precomposing more than one layer.

297

30. Repeat steps 26 to 29 for the remaining pairs of layers. When completed, your Time Layout window should look like the following figure.

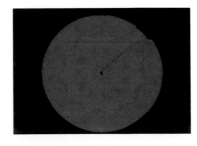

Now it's time to animate each layer by rotating its anchor point. It would be a good time to save your project.

31. Turn off all layers except yellow.

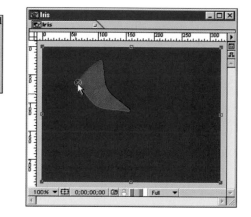

TIP

Press the hotkey Y on your keyboard to select the Pan Behind tool.

NOTE

While the After Effects User Guide calls it the Pan Behind tool, you (and everyone else in the world) probably know it as the Anchor Point tool.

It is important to note that the Composition, Time Layout, or Layer window must be the active window for this tool to be active. If the Project window is the active window, the "Y" key command will not work.

TIP

Press the hotkey W to select the Rotate tool.

298

32. Select the Pan Behind tool and move the anchor point to the bottom-left edge of the iris blade to get the proper rotation.

33. Test the new anchor point placement by switching to the Rotate tool and rotating the layer. Once you're done testing (and you're happy with the movement), put it back the way it was. A simple Undo command will work fine.

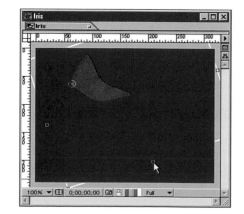

34. When you have the anchor point in the proper position for a realistic rotation, follow steps 31–33 until each of the colors has a new anchor point location.

TIP

You may find it helpful to look at the final movie (located in the folder for this chapter on the Book CD) to see exactly what you are creating.

TIP

You may want to turn each layer's video on individually to make the placement of the anchor point a bit easier.

Also, placing your anchor points to the far outside edge seems to work better in getting them fully out of the circle when they rotate away.

35. Drag another copy of iris textured.tga from the Project window onto the top of the Time Layout window.

36. Double-click on the layer to open its Layer window.

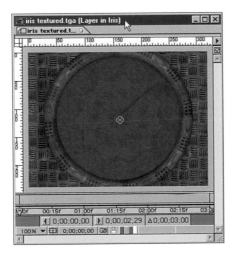

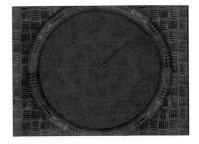

37. Use the Oval Mask tool to drag out a mask over the iris section and then adjust the position of the mask using the Selection Tool.

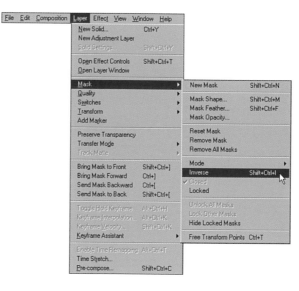

300

38. Go to Layer➡Mask➡Inverse. This cuts out the hole you'll be looking through when the iris opens. Close the Layer window when done.

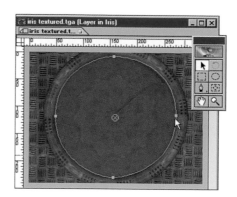

39. Turn off the video for all of the layers except layers 1 and 2 (the newly added iris textured.tga and yellow).

40. Select the yellow color layer and open its Rotation value.

41. At 0:00, set a keyframe by clicking on the Rotation stopwatch.

42. Press O on your keyboard to go to the Out point of this layer.

43. Rotate the layer until it disappears behind the portal frame of the iris textured.tga layer (in this example, the value is -104.0 degrees).

Now make a RAM preview and check the motion. If it looks the way you want it to, move on to the next steps. If not, go back and tweak some of your rotation degrees. Now would be a good time to save your project.

NOTE

RAM previews are meant to show portions of the composition rather than the entire thing, and how much you'll see depends on how much free RAM you have. For this reason, be sure to temporarily adjust your composition's Work Area Markers before creating a RAM preview. The quickest method is to set the Current Time marker at the desired beginning frame, press the hotkey B, move the marker to the desired ending frame, and press the hotkey N.

With the beginning point and end point set for the Work Area, there are two methods for creating a RAM preview. You can go to Window, Show Time Controls (or press Ctrl+3 on the PC or Cmd+3 on the Mac) and click the arrow button on the far-right side of the Time Controls box. Or, you can press 0 on your keyboard's numeric keypad. Tough choice, huh?

301

TIP

If you hold down the Shift key while making a RAM preview, After Effects will only cache *every other frame*. This trick can be a huge timesaver, especially if the only reason you are making a RAM preview is to check the basic motion of your layers.

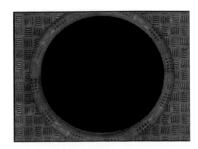

44. Once the rotation is to your liking, you can copy and paste rotation keyframes from one color layer to all the rest. Click once on Rotation so that both of the Rotation keyframes are highlighted in the Time Layout window.

45. Go up to the Edit menu and choose Copy.

TIP

Press Ctrl+C on the PC or Cmd+C on the Mac while the keyframes are highlighted to copy the keyframes. Then press Ctrl+V on the PC or the Cmd+V on Mac to paste the keys.

302

TIP

After you have pasted in all of your keyframes, you can select all of the remaining layers and press R to reveal the new rotation keyframes.

After you have viewed the new rotation keyframes, press R again to hide the rotation properties.

46. Make sure your Time Marker is at 0:00 in the Time Layout window. Then select each of the remaining colors one at a time and paste the keyframes by choosing Edit➡Paste.

47. Drag star burst.avi from the Project window onto the very bottom of the Time Layout window.

48. Turn on the visibility of all layers and make another RAM preview to see how everything works together.

49. You want to add drop shadows for perspective and contrast between the iris blades. Select yellow and go to Effect➡Perspective➡Drop Shadow.

50. Adjust Opacity to about 75%, Distance to 8.5, and Softness to 9.

51. Copy and paste this effect to add a Drop Shadow to all of the color layers. Once you've pasted the Drop Shadow onto all of the color layers, select each of them in the Time Layout window and press E to reveal the effect.

Make another RAM preview. If you're happy with the rotation and drop shadow of each of your blades, it's time to render your final movie with all the correct settings for your appropriate output and/or distribution method. Now would be a good time to save your project.

52. With the current Composition or Time Layout window as the active window, or with the Composition's name/icon selected in the Project window, go up to your menu bar and select Composition–Make Movie.

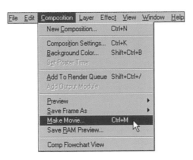

53. A Save Movie As dialog box will open. Save the movie as Iris to your desired folder or directory.

54. The Render Queue opens next. Here you need to change Render Settings from Current Settings to Best Settings.

55. Next, click on the underlined Output Module setting and change the output module to your choice of format. Check "Import into project when done" so you can quickly see your movie once it's finished rendering.

56. In the same Output Module Settings dialog box, click on the Format Options button in the Video Output section.

57. The Compression Settings dialog box pops up. For this example, choose Sorenson Video for your compressor and set it to Best Quality. Click OK when done.

58. When the Render Queue is finally ready, click Render.

After the render is complete, play your movie to make sure it came out the way you expected. If all is well, save your final project as Opening Iris.

The raw artwork supplied for this chapter was created using Discreet 3D Studio MAX, Adobe Photoshop, and Adobe After Effects.

CHAPTER

16

Creating an Animated Station ID

This technique is a mainstay of all network programming. It is used to identify a particular station or network to the viewer.

If you have a TV, you've seen them... the little logos in the bottom-right corner that identify what station you're watching (and ruin the videotape you're making for your personal "Best of the WWF Body Slams" collection). Frequently, clients will ask to have these logos included in their videos for quick recognition and/or copyright protection. With After Effects, you can satisfy your clients' wishes with a few quick mouse clicks.

1. Open a new project by clicking File➡New➡New Project.

2. Create a new composition by choosing Composition➡New Composition.

TIP

You can also create a new composition by pressing Ctrl+N on the PC or Cmd+N on the Mac.

3. In the New Composition dialog box, animate your text in a 320×240 composition window because this will be the size of your finished movie. You're going to work at 15 frames per second, with a duration of 5 seconds. Name it Station ID.

4. To add the video footage you will be using, choose File➡Import➡Footage Files.

TIP

You can also import multiple footage files by doing the following:

PC—Right-click in the project window or press Ctrl+Alt+I.
Mac—Hold down the Ctrl key and click in the project window, or press Command+Option+I.

NOTE

The Macintosh version of After Effects cannot select multiple files and import them at once. Mac users will need to import these files one at a time; that is, select one file and then click open, select the next and click open, and so on until finally clicking Done when finished.

Also, your Mac system may convert the .avi file when importing. This is fine and will not affect your playback or rendering.

5. Select both energyTV.mov and orbitz.mov in the Artwork folder for this chapter.

Now that you've imported the movie files that you plan to use for this project, it's time to move it from the Project window to the Time Layout window. You will also set one of the imported movie files to loop. Now would be a good time to save your project.

6. The orbitz.mov file is too short for your current composition, so you need to make it loop. With this file selected in the Project window, go to File➟Interpret Footage➟Main.

NOTE

If you get the Interpret Footage dialog box after selecting orbitz.mov, choose "Guess" and click OK to continue with the tutorial.

TIP

As a general rule, it's always a good idea to save your project periodically throughout the creative process. This will save you many headaches in the long run. It's also a good idea to save your project with different names throughout the process (project a, project b, project c, etc.). This way you can go back a few steps if you see that your experimentation has taken you in a different direction than where you want to end up.

TIP

You can also press Ctrl+F on the PC or Cmd+F on the Mac.

311

NOTE
The alpha channel is necessary to complete this effect.

7. This movie file has an alpha channel, so click Treat As Straight and change Looping from 1 to 2. Click OK when done.

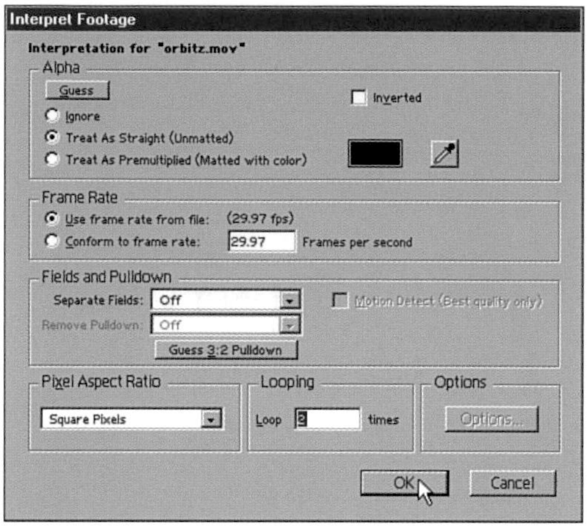

TIP
Another way to duplicate the layer is to press Ctrl+D on the PC or Cmd+D on the Mac.

8. Drag energyTV.mov onto the Time Layout window. Duplicate it by going to Edit➡Duplicate.

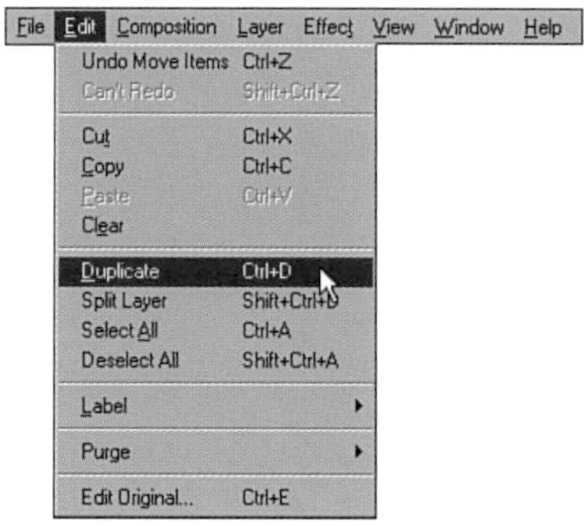

NOTE
Because you've looped orbitz.mov, you'll see that its layer duration bar actually runs past the end of the comp. Don't worry, that's okay.

9. Drag orbitz.mov onto the Time Layout window. Your Time Layout window should now look like the following figure.

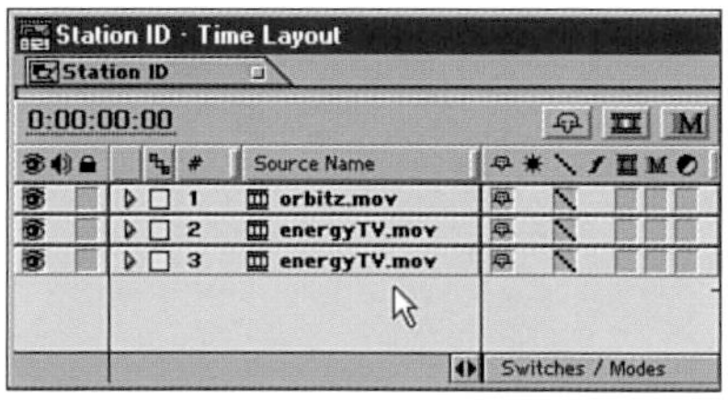

10. Turn on Title➡Action Safe Guides to check the placement of the animated spheres. You want them to stay within the Action Safe area throughout the composition.

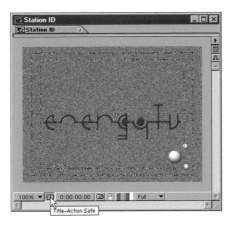

11. Toggle Switches/Modes to Modes.

12. Select layer 2 and change its Transfer Mode from Normal to Overlay. Also change its TrkMat (track matte) from No Track Matte to Alpha Matte "orbitz.mov". Don't worry that the top two layers have disappeared; they will return in a couple more steps.

NOTE

Track Matte sets up a matte and fill relation-ship between two layers positioned one on top of the other in the layer stack. Once enabled the Track Matte allows the bottom layer to show through areas of the top layer based on the top layer's alpha or luminance values.

An Alpha matte allows the bottom layer to show through areas of the top layer that have alpha channel pixel values of greater than 0%. Areas that have alpha channel pixel values of 100% will appear completely opaque, and those with values between 1% and 99% appear semitrans-parent.

A Luma matte allows the bottom layer to show through areas of the top layer that have luminance values of greater than 0%. Areas that have luminance values of 100% will appear completely opaque, and those with values between 1% and 99% appear semitransparent.

313

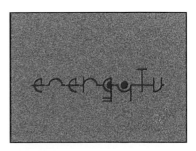

The Pre-compose feature of After Effects can help you organize projects, speed up previews, and generally work more efficiently. In this particular case, you will use Pre-compose to group layers together and then apply an effect to the new group.

TIP

You can also pre-compose by pressing Ctrl+Shift+C on the PC or Cmd+Shift+C on the Mac.

13. Select layers 1 and 2. Go to Layer➡Pre-compose.

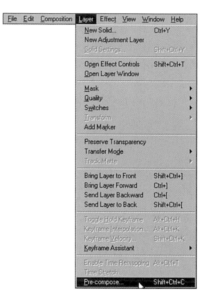

NOTE

"Move all attributes into the new composition" is selected by default because we are precomposing more than one layer.

14. Name it orbitz PC so you know it's both layers combined, make sure Move all attributes into the new composition is selected, and click OK.

314

15. While the orbitz PC layer is selected on the Time Layout window, go to Effect➡Perspective➡Bevel Alpha. Notice that the animated spheres have reappeared in your main comp window.

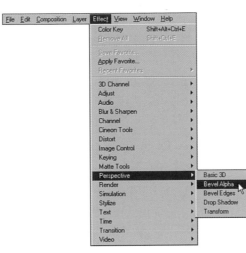

16. In the Effect Controls window, change the Edge Thickness setting to about 3.5 and leave the other settings at their defaults.

315

17. Go to Effect➡Perspective➡Drop Shadow.

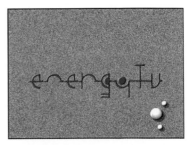

316

18. Change the shadow's Opacity to 70% and Softness to about 8.

Make a RAM preview. If you are happy with the location of the Station ID logo and matte effect, it's time to render your final movie with all the correct settings for your appropriate output and/or distribution method. Now would be a good time to save your project.

19. With the current Composition or Time Layout window as the active window, or with the Composition's name/icon selected in the Project window, go up to your menu bar and select Composition➡Make Movie.

20. A Save Movie As dialog box will open. Save the movie as Station ID to your desired folder or directory.

21. The Render Queue will open next. Here you need to change Render Settings from Current Settings to Best Settings.

22. Next, click on the underlined Output Module setting and change the output module to your choice of format. Check "Import into project when done" so you can quickly see your movie once it's finished rendering.

317

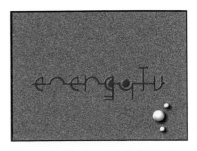

23. In the same Output Module Settings dialog box, click on the Format Options button in the Video Output section.

24. The Compression Settings dialog box pops. For this example, choose Sorenson Video for your compressor and set it to Best Quality. Click OK when you are done.

TIP

If you checked the "Import into project when done" check box in the Output Module, simply double-click on the movie icon in your Project window.

TIP

If you plan on sharing your project file with others, especially cross-platform, you need to add the .aep extension to your project name.

25. When the Render Queue is finally ready, click Render.

After the render is complete, play your movie to make sure it came out the way you expected. If all is well, save your final project as Station ID.

The raw artwork supplied for this chapter was created using Adobe Photoshop and Discreet 3D Studio Max.

CHAPTER
17

Revealing an Image in a Smoky/Watery Haze

This technique could be used to create a nice introduction to a television program or a corporate logo ID. It can also be used to create a haze for any type of project.

Third-party plug-in packages are expensive. I realize I have a gift for stating the obvious, but if you bought every After Effects plug-in available, you'd probably spend over $20,000. Books like this one can help by providing demo plug-ins (look on your Goodies CD), but sometimes it's necessary to do things the old-fashioned (cheap) way.

In this chapter, you'll create a video clip of an ancient Easter Island monolith serenely bathing in a hidden lagoon. Unfortunately, the original atmosphere of the clip is too pristine to be considered mysterious, so you'll want to add some smokiness without having to break your budget buying a smoke filter package. This project will "reveal" the hidden lagoon through the use of blob-like alpha mattes created in Photoshop.

1. Open a new project by clicking File➡New➡New Project.

2. Create a new composition by choosing Composition➡New Composition.

3. In the Composition Settings dialog box, animate your logo in a 320×240 composition window because this will be the size of your finished movie. You're going to work at 15 frames per second, with a duration of 4 seconds. Name it Pacific Mysteries and click OK when you're done.

TIP

You can also create a new composition by pressing Ctrl+N on the PC or Cmd+N on the Mac.

4. To add the blurry images you'll be using as mattes, choose File➡Import➡Photoshop As Comp.

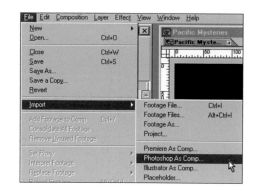

5. Navigate to the Artwork folder for this chapter and select blurs.psd. Click Open.

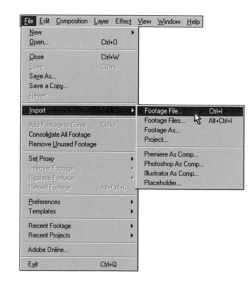

322

TIP

You can also import footage by doing the following:

PC—Right-clicking in the project window, or using the Ctrl+I hotkey combination.
Mac—Holding down the Ctrl key and clicking in the project window, or using the Cmd+I hotkey combination.

Or you can simply double click inside the Project window in the white area (not on a file).

6. Next, you need to import the video you'll be using. Do this by selecting File➡Import➡Footage File.

7. Now choose Easter.mov in the Open dialog box.

8. Finally, you need to add a moving layer to use as a displacement layer for the haze you'll be making. So follow the previous steps to import displacer.mov.

323

Now that you have all the materials ready, let's put them in the correct order in the Time Layout window and begin to give them a little life. You'll also scale a layer and apply a displacement map before actually creating and animating the haze that will eventually reveal your monolith. Now would also be a good time to save your project.

Applying Adobe After Effects Studio Techniques

TIP

As a general rule, it's always a good idea to save your project periodically throughout the creative process. This will save you many headaches in the long run. It's also a good idea to save your project with different names throughout the process (project a, project b, project c, etc.). This way you can go back a few steps if you see that your experimentation has taken you in a different direction than where you want to end up.

9. Drag the Easter Island video layer (Easter.mov) onto the Time Layout window. Notice the rectangular outline shape of the file as you drag it onto the Time Layout window.

10. When properly placed in the Time Layout window, the Easter Island video layer automatically centers itself in the Composition window.

324

11. Open the blurs.psd folder at the top of your project window and select the blur1/blurs.psd layer.

12. Drag the blur1/blurs.psd file and place it in the Time Layout window.

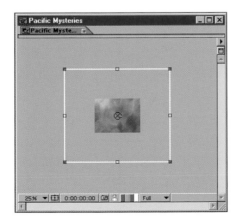

13. You'll want to scale your blur1/blurs.psd layer to make sure it completely covers your Easter.mov video layer. About 200% works well here.

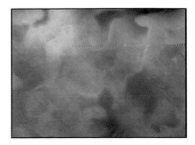

NOTE

New layers are placed at the top of the stack in the Time Layout window, so the blur1/blurs.psd file is automatically placed above the Easter.mov video layer. This is exactly where you want it.

NOTE

There are two simple ways to scale a layer:

- Select the layer, type the letter S on your keyboard, click on the number value, and change it to whatever value serves you best.

- Select the layer, look up in the Composition window, and drag the layer handles to whatever size serves you best.

For more information, please consult the After Effects User Manual or the Help menu.

14. In order to bring life to this layer (and all the other haze layers), you need to use a displacement map. It's time to add displacer.mov to the Time Layout window. You won't actually see this layer in your final movie, so place it at the very bottom of the layer stack.

15. Select the blur1 layer in either the Comp or Time Layout window. Then go to Effect➡Distort➡Displacement Map.

If you decide to use a different video layer, be sure to check which variable in the Max Vertical and Max Horizontal Displacement drop-down list gives you the best results. Experiment freely!

16. In the Displacement Map Effect Controls window, select displacer.mov as the Displacement Map Layer. Also select Lightness in the "Use For Horizontal Displacement" pulldown menu. Leave the Max Vertical and Max Horizontal Displacement values set to their default settings (5).

326

In the next several steps, you'll begin creating and animating the haze openings that eventually reveal the idol in the secluded pond. Now would be a good time to save your project.

17. Okay, it's time to add a little mystery to your video. Select the remaining blurs from the blurs.psd folder in the Project window and drag them into the Time Layout window.

18. Once they're in the Time Layout window, select the Easter.mov layer and duplicate it twice by pressing Ctrl+D on the PC or Cmd+D on the Mac. Place each of the *new* Easter.mov layers beneath a blur layer.

327

19. Move the current time marker to the last frame in the Time Layout window, and then select the blur2 layer. Alt+drag on the PC or Option+drag on the Mac until it's over the central object of the video layer—the statue.

TIP

Alt+drag on the PC or Option+drag on the Mac to see the layer in full color as you drag it, instead of just seeing its bounding box or layer handles.

TIP

Alt+shift+P on the PC or Opt+P on the Mac also sets a keyframe for position at the current value.

NOTE

Although it obscures the object now, after you set the video to use this blur layer as its alpha matte, the area covered by the blur will be the only portion of the layer that is visible.

328

20. Set a keyframe for position by selecting the blur2 layer, pressing P, and clicking on the stopwatch.

21. Move the current time marker back two seconds in the Time Layout window to the 2:00 mark.

22. Now move the blur2 layer slightly away from the center of the screen. This will represent the haze opening slightly. The less motion you create, the more realistic it will appear to be.

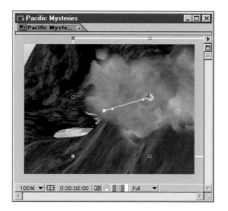

NOTE

Note that when repeating the steps for the blur3 layer that the layer is obscured by the Easter.mov layer. By selecting the layer in the Time Layout window, its handles become selected in the Comp window and that is how to tell which layer is being altered.

23. Notice that a new Position keyframe is set automatically.

24. Repeat steps 19 through 21 for the remaining blur (blur3), but move it in a different direction away from the center. You'll want to stagger the keyframes on the timeline to keep things from appearing mechanical.

TIP

To select and stagger the keyframes along the timeline, click on the word Position to select both of the Position keyframes and then click and drag to shift them along the timeline.

25. Toggle Switches/Modes to Modes. Notice how the third column changes from Switches to Modes.

NOTE

An alpha matte is used to reveal only the portions of the layer below (in this case, easter.mov) that fall within the alpha channel of the layer above (in this case, blur2/blurs.psd). The alpha channel for the blur layer, as defined in the Photoshop file, acts like a matte placed over the easter.mov video layer. The blur layer's video is turned off (notice the eye in the switches panel), and there is now a dotted line between this layer and the easter.mov layer directly below it. This indicates that there is now a track matte relationship between them. If another layer is placed between them in the stack, this relationship will be disrupted.

329

26. Toggle the TrkMat (track matte) for the Easter.mov on layer 2 from None to Alpha Matte blur2/blurs.psd.

330

27. Select 'Alpha Matte blur3/blurs.psd' from the TrkMat pulldown menu for the Easter.mov on layer 4.

Make a RAM preview. You'll see that solid bits of empty space are moving through the haze (which is a rare sight in nature). You can fix this by keyframing the opacity of the blur layers, giving the final rendered image a much more organic look. Now would be a good time to save your project.

28. Select the blur2/blurs.psd layer and press the letter T on your keyboard to open the opacity property.

29. Press the End key on your keyboard to jump to the end of your Time Layout window. Then click on the underlined Opacity value (currently set to 100%) and set the blur2/blurs.psd layer's opacity to around 44%. Finally, set this as a keyframe by clicking on the Opacity stopwatch icon. The following figure shows the Opacity dialog box that you get by clicking on the Opacity percentage value.

30. Move the current time marker back about two seconds and lower the opacity to 0% for the same layer.

31. Now select both keyframes (either by marqueeing them in the Time Layout window or by clicking once on Opacity) and copy these keyframes by pressing Ctrl+C on the PC or Cmd+C on the Mac.

32. Select the blur3/blurs.psd layer, and then paste these keyframes onto the opacity of the blur3/blurs.psd layer by opening its Opacity property and pressing Ctrl+V on the PC or Cmd+V on the Mac.

33. Deselect all keyframes by clicking anywhere in the white area. Then click and drag the 0% keyframe on the blur3 layer (and *only* the 0% keyframe) to stagger the effect. Dragging it 10 to 15 frames should be sufficient.

TIP

Alt+P on the PC or Opt+T on the Mac also sets a keyframe for Opacity at the current value.

NOTE

The Current Time Marker should still be set to the 2-second mark. If it isn't, you've been naughty and you should move it back to the 2-second mark before doing step 32.

NOTE

You may want to play with the amount of movement in your blur layers, as well as how much they intersect. I've left an area in the middle where they don't intersect so that there's always a wisp of haze on the central object.

331

If you render a RAM preview at this point, you'll notice that the central haze appears to part more realistically.

The next several steps are for fine-tuning the effect to your liking, so use them as guidelines and feel free to experiment with the settings until you get the look you're after. Now would be a good time to save your project.

TIP

Currently you have no effects applied to the two upper blur layers, so you need to select the Effect name Displacement Map and press Ctrl+c on the PC or Cmd+c on the Mac to copy the effect from within the Effect Controls window. Then select one of the blur layers in the Time Layout window (start with blur2), and press Ctrl+v on the PC or Cmd+v on the Mac to paste the effect here. In the Effect Controls window, a new tab appears showing the effect applied to the layer. For any additional effects in this same layer, simply copy and paste right in this window without going to the timeline.

TIP

A quick way to check that everything was pasted in correctly is that after pasting the effects, select the layer in the Time Layout window and press E to reveal the effects applied to that layer. Notice that Displacement Map appears under both of the blur2 and blur3 layers.

332

34. You can make the haze even better by adding more displacement effects. The quickest way is to go to the Effect Controls window and copy and paste the Displacement Map effect from blur1/blurs.psd to the other two blur layers. (Read the Tip if you're unsure how to do this.) Be sure to paste the Displacement Map effect into both the blur2/blurs.psd and blur3/blurs.psd layers.

35. Now you just have to make sure that the Displacement Map Layer in each layer is set to use displacer.mov.

Make a RAM preview. Things look a little bit better, but if you animate the amount of displacement on the blurs, you'll see a greater improvement.

36. Go to the final frame of the composition by pressing the End key on your keyboard. You want to set a keyframe for the Max Horizontal Displacement on the blur2/blurs.psd layer. The quickest way to do this is to Alt+click the value name (in this case, Max Horizontal Displacement) on the PC or Option+click it on the Mac.

37. Now repeat step 36 for the Max Vertical Displacement on the blur2/blurs.psd layer.

38. Now that the keyframes are set, you need to adjust the value of the Max Vertical Displacement on the blur2/blurs.psd layer. You can do this by adjusting the Max Vertical Displacement slider in the Effects Control window, or by clicking on the numeric value in the Time Layout window (as shown in the following figure). In this example I have chosen a value of 9.4, but please don't feel you need to be too precise about this step. You just want to keep things from appearing to be static.

NOTE

In order to go above 100 for the Max Horizontal Displacement or Max Vertical Displacement, you must click on the underlined numeric value in the Effects Control Window or in the Time Layout window.

Make another RAM preview. You'll see that the openings appear to be more organic.

---

39. Finally, you need to add a fast blur to soften the edges of the blur2 and blur3 layers. First, select the blur2/blurs.psd and blur3/blurs.psd layers and choose Effect➡Blur & Sharpen➡Fast Blur.

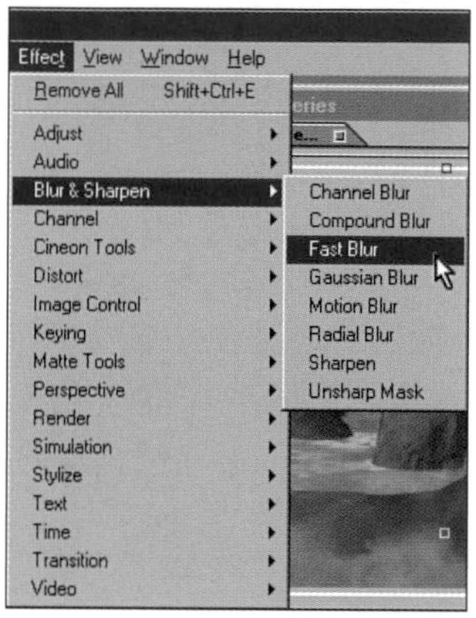

40. Set the fast Blur to around 10, with blur dimensions on both horizontal and vertical.

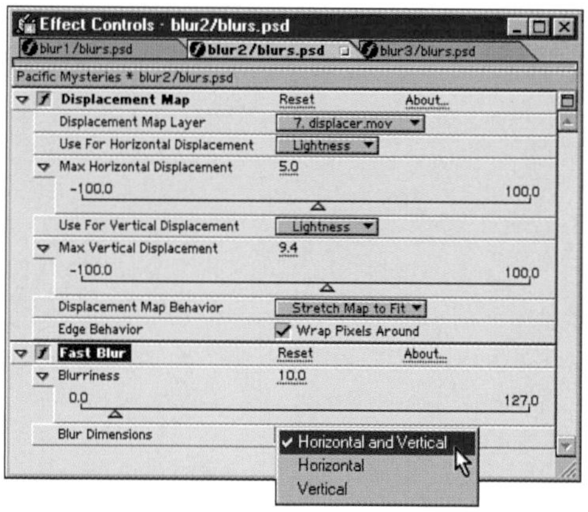

It's time to render your final movie with all the correct settings for your appropriate output and/or distribution method. Now would be a good time to save your project.

---

41. Now you can make your movie. With the current Composition or Time Layout window as the active window, or with the Composition's name/icon selected in the Project window, go up to your menu bar and select Composition➡Make Movie.

TIP

You can also do the Make Movie command by pressing Ctrl+M on the PC or Cmd+M on the Mac.

42. A Save Movie As dialog box opens. Save the movie as Pacific Mysteries to your desired folder or directory.

335

43. The Render Queue opens next. Here you need to change Render Settings from Current Settings to Best Settings.

44. Next, click on the underlined Output Module setting and change the output module to your choice of format. Check "Import into project when done" so you can quickly see your movie once it's finished rendering.

45. In the same Output Module Settings dialog box, click on the Format Options button in the Video Output section.

46. The Compression Settings dialog box pops up. For this example, choose Sorenson Video for your compressor and set it at Best Quality. Click OK when done.

47. When the Render Queue is finally ready, click Render.

TIP

If you checked the "Import into project when done" checkbox in the Output Module, simply double-click on the movie icon in your Project window.

TIP

If you plan on sharing your project file with others, especially cross-platform, you need to add the .aep extension to your project name.

After the render is complete, play your movie to make sure it came out the way you expected. If all is well, save your final project as Pacific Mysteries.

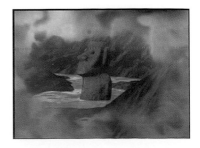

Part IX

Evolution Effects

CHAPTER
18

Casting Shadows in 3D Space with the Atomic Power Multiplane Plug-In

This technique and style of animation is used by nearly all cartoon television shows and many of the animated films you see in movie theaters. If you have a good idea for a cartoon series, this is a very good (and inexpensive) way of producing your own pilot episode.

In this chapter, you'll create (and work in) 3-dimensional space within After Effects using a technique called *Multiplaning*. The term is derived from the Multiplane camera developed by the Disney Animation Studio to create the illusion of depth in the otherwise two-dimensional world of cell animation. The original (and very large) Multiplane camera suspended flat images on panes of glass beneath the camera so that it could pull focus from one plane to another, or pan across the scene for a realistic parallax effect.

Previously in After Effects, the only way to create the look of 3D space was to keyframe multiple parameters within the Time Layout window, splitting layers and painstakingly fine-tuning the scene. Now the Multiplane tool, part of the Evolution filter set from Atomic Power Corporation (**www.AtomicPower.com**), takes much of the work out of setting up a Multiplane scene.

In this chapter, you'll learn how install and use the Multiplane plug-in, set up your layers in true 3D space, add depth and motion to a layered Illustrator file, and cast shadows only on the appropriate layer.

1. First you need to install the Multiplane plug-in. Navigate to the Plug-ins folder for this chapter on the book CD-ROM and open it (you can also find it in the Atomic Power folder on the Goodies CD). This is where you'll find the Multiplane filter.

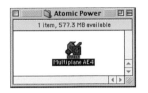

2. Copy the Multiplane filter to your Adobe After Effects 4.0/4.1 Plug-ins folder/directory. If you're currently running After Effects, quit out of the application. When you relaunch After Effects, the Multiplane filter will be initialized. (If you don't initialize the filter, it won't show up in your Effects menu.)

3. Open a new project by selecting File➜New➜New Project.

| File | Edit | Composition | Layer | Effect | View | Window | Help |

> **NOTE**
>
> All of the Illustrator layers have been set up to be read by After Effects when we import them. Now you will animate these layers adding motion and depth using the Multi-Plane plug-in.

4. Import the Illustrator file keeping all of its layers intact by choosing File➡Import➡Illustrator as Comp.

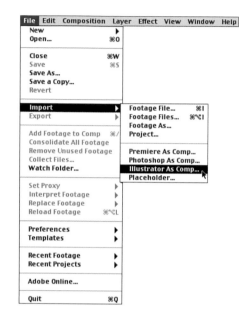

5. Navigate to the Artwork folder for this chapter and select Landscape.ai. Click Open.

6. You now have two items in your Project window: a folder and a composition, both named Landscape.ai. Click on the triangle next to the folder named Landscape.ai. It now displays the contents of the folder.

7. There is one additional video file you need to add to the project. Choose File➡Import➡Footage File.

> **TIP**
>
> You can also import footage by doing the following:
>
> PC—Right-click in the project window, or press Ctrl+I.
> Mac—Hold down the Ctrl key and click in the project window, or press Cmd+I.

8. Now select Tractor.mov in the Artwork folder for this chapter and click Open.

343

Now that you've imported the Illustrator file with all three of its layers and the additional animated movie clip, it's time to work with them in the After Effects Time Layout window. You'll be adding motion and effects to these layers using the Multiplane plug-in. Now would be a good time to save your project.

344

9. Double-click on the Landscape.ai composition near the bottom of your Project window. This will open the Time Layout window and the Composition window.

10. All of the Illustrator layers now appear as composition layers in the After Effects Time Layout window in their correct order.

11. Even though After Effects kept the Illustrator graphic size correct at 440×253, it's not the size you want for your composition. Go to Composition➡Composition Settings and set Frame Size to 320×240, Frame Rate to 15, and Duration to 15 seconds. Click OK when you're done.

12. The next thing you need to do before you begin animating your layers is change each layer's Quality level from Draft to Best. You can do this by clicking once on each of the dotted backslash lines to turn them into solid forward-slash lines.

NOTE

When you import a file as a composition from either Photoshop or Illustrator, After Effects will set the frame rate and duration to what you used for the last comp created. Always make sure you check your Composition Settings when you're done importing a file as a composition.

TIP

You can also simply click and drag down the layer stack over each of the layers' Quality switches to change them all as you go.

13. Look carefully at the layer named Sky (layer 3). It should contain banding (vertical and/or horizontal lines), which can occur in gradients that are imported from Illustrator into After Effects.

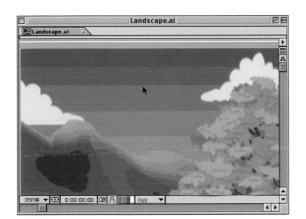

345

14. To fix the banding problem, select the Sky layer in the Project window.

15. Go to File➡Interpret Footage➡Main.

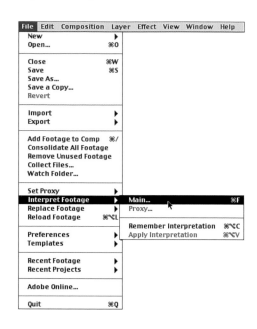

16. Click the Options button in the bottom-right corner of the Interpret Footage dialog box.

NOTE

After you set the Interpret Footage Antialiasing command to More Accurate, don't panic if you find that the gradient layer has been cut off at either the top or bottom (as if a mask was added). Just set your Quality setting back to Draft. This is a bug that occurs on some After Effects systems. Hopefully this quirk will be fixed in the next version.

17. Change Antialiasing from Faster to More Accurate. Click OK twice to get back to the Project window.

18. Now drag Tractor.mov from the Project menu to the Time Layout window.

19. In the Time Layout window, make Tractor.mov layer 2 by dragging it between the Tree layer (layer 1) and the Hills layer (layer 3).

Now that you have all of the source layers arranged in the Time Layout window, they should show up in the Composition window in the order they're meant to appear in your scene. However, the scene is very flat, so you'll now add drop shadows and animate layers and camera positions within Multiplane to create a sense of depth between the layers. Now would be a good time to save your project.

20. Make sure that your Time Marker is at 0:00 and create a new layer by going to Layer→New Solid.

TIP

You can also create a new solid by pressing Ctrl+Y on the PC or Cmd+Y on the Mac.

21. Since your composition will involve a camera move, the original Illustrator graphic layers and movie clip were created larger than your final output size (see step 11, where you made the change). However, you want your new solid layer to match your graphic layers, so set the size to 440×253 pixels. Name your new solid Multiplane and click OK. The color of the Solid does not matter.

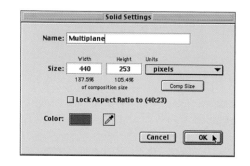

22. Your new layer will appear in the Time Layout window as the top layer. Drag the Multiplane layer to the bottom of the Time Layout window.

When you use the Multiplane filter in a scene, it's applied to a blank (or solid) layer. Then, all layers that will be controlled by the Multiplane filter are imported and assigned default depth placement on the Z-axis.

In plain English this means that the layers will be assigned their depth by selecting them from within the Multiplane filter, rather than by applying the filter to each layer individually.

23. With the Multiplane layer still selected, apply the Multiplane filter by choosing Effect➡Evolution➡Multiplane 4.

24. You will now assign each layer in the Time Layout window to a layer in the Multiplane Effect Controls window.

25. Go to Layer 1 in the Effect Controls window and click on the arrow next to it. To the right of the Layer parameter name is the drop-down menu, which currently reads 5. Multiplane. Click on the layer selection drop-down menu and notice that all of the layers in you composition are listed there. Select "1. Tree".

26. Close Layer 1 by clicking the arrow next to it and go to Layer 2 in the Effect Controls window. Click on the arrow next to Layer 2 to open the controls. To the right of the Layer parameter name is the drop-down menu, which currently reads None. Click on the layer selection drop-down menu and select 2. Tractor.mov.

349

27. Close Layer 2 and go to Layer 3 in the Effect Controls window. Click on the arrow next to Layer 3 to open the controls. To the right of the Layer parameter name is the drop-down menu, which currently reads None. Click on the layer selection drop-down menu and select 3. Hills.

28. Close Layer 3 and go to Layer 4 in the Effect Controls window. Click on the arrow next to Layer 4 to open the controls. To the right of the Layer parameter name is the drop-down menu, which currently reads None. Click on the layer selection drop-down menu and select 4. Sky.

NOTE

You will need .o twirl down (click the arrows next to) the previous layers' 1-3 controls again to see each one's depth setting because you collapsed them earlier in the chapter.

29. Note that each layer is automatically assigned a Depth position. Layer 1 is 10 units from the camera, Layer 2 is 20 units from the camera, Layer 3 is 30 units from the camera, and Layer 4 is 40 units from the camera.

30. Now go to the Time Layout window and turn off the visibility (video switch) for all layers except the Multiplane layer (Layer 5).

31. Notice that the layers were all the same size when you started, but they now appear to be out of scale because of their new depth positions.

32. For this composition, you don't want the layers to be scaled. To quickly fix this, go back to the Effect Controls window and open the Camera parameters.

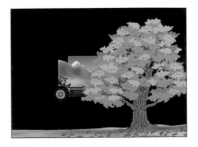

33. Deselect Depth Scaling.

34. All of your layers should now appear to be the correct size in the Composition window.

Although your layers still appear as one flat image, they're positioned in depth along the Z-axis at 10, 20, 30, and 40 units from the camera, respectively. You'll see later in the chapter why this is important for controlling shadows between layers. Now would be a good time to save your project.

35. Go to the Effect Controls window and open the Shadows parameters. You may want to collapse the Camera parameters to give yourself more room.

36. Click on the Enable Shadows check box.

NOTE

When the Enable Shadows function is enabled within the Multiplane plug-in, each layer has the ability to cast shadows on the layer behind it.

When you select the Cast Shadows option for any layer, it will cast shadows based on the position of the light with respect to the layers in your composition.

37. Close the Shadows parameters in the Effect Controls window and open the Layer 1 (Tree) parameters. Enable Cast Shadows.

NOTE

You are now going to make adjustments to the Multiplane controls and set some keyframes in the Time Layout window.

353

38. In the Time Layout window, make sure that Multiplane (layer 5) is still selected. Press the letter E on your keyboard to display the Multiplane 4 effect.

39. Click once on the Multiplane 4 arrow to display the parameters for the Multiplane 4 effect.

354

40. Make sure that the Time Marker is positioned at 0:00 and set a position keyframe for Tractor.mov by opening Layer 2 and clicking on the Position stopwatch icon.

41. Move the Time Marker to the end of your composition (the 15-second mark) by pressing the End key on your keyboard.

42. Click once on the Position values (they probably read 220.0, 126.5) to open up the Multiplane Position settings dialog box.

43. Change the position value for the X-axis from 220.0 to 800.0 (make sure you're looking at pixel units). This will add a second keyframe and make the tractor travel from left to right through the scene.

44. Now it's time to make some shadows! In the Effect Control window, open the Shadows control settings.

NOTE

You can also click on the crosshairs and play with the position of the light in the Composition window to create the exact shadow position you desire. You may have to zoom out of your Composition window to be able to see the position of the light.

You need to have the Multiplane 4 effect name selected in the Effect Controls window to see the Light Position point control in the comp window.

TIP

The color and pattern of the shadow are based on the color and pattern of the layer that's casting the shadow. When you turn up the Shadow Saturation value, it creates a stained-glass effect by causing the light to appear to shine through the layers onto the layers behind them. If you turn this parameter up for the Tree layer, you'll see the orange and yellow leaves within the Tree's shadow.

356

45. Click once on the Light Position values (they probably read 220.0, 126.5) to open up the Light Position settings dialog box.

46. Change the Light Position value to 275 pixels for the X-axis and –60 pixels for the Y-axis. Click OK when done.

47. To soften the edge of the Tree layer shadow, click on the underlined Shadows Softness value in the Effect Controls window and type in the value (or move the slider to) 1.5. A little softness will automatically add a feeling of depth to your scene.

Notice that the Tree shadow is falling evenly on all layers. This should not happen if the layers are truly positioned in Z-space. The way to limit the shadow to the Tractor layer is to position the Hills and Sky layers further back in the scene so the Tree shadow doesn't fall on them.

48. In the Effect Controls window, close the Shadows controls and open the Sky layer (Layer 4) and click once on the Depth value (it probably reads 40) to open up the Depth Slider Control dialog box.

TIP

This may be easier to see if the tractor is in the shadow too. Move the time marker to about 3:00 to view.

49. Set Depth to 350.

50. Now go to the Hills layer (Layer 3) and set Depth to 300.

357

NOTE

The shadow color is determined by the Ambient Light setting. By default, this shadow color is gray when the Shadow Saturation parameter has a low setting. The Ambient Light parameter allows you to select any color for the shadow. This is very useful when you have to match existing shadows in footage or graphic elements.

The Tree layer shadow now barely falls on the Hills layer, and the edge of the shadow is much softer on the Hills layer than on the Tractor layer.

The last little polish that this project needs is to add a camera move. In the next few steps, if you find that you want to preview the camera move more quickly, simply turn off the Tree layer shadow until you've finished the camera move. Now would be a good time to save your project.

51. In the Time Layout window, move the Time Marker to the 5-second mark.

52. In the Time Layout window, open the Camera parameter under Multiplane 4.

53. Click on the Camera Position stopwatch.

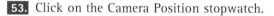

54. Move the Time Marker to the end of your composition (the 15-second mark) by pressing the End key on your keyboard.

55. Click once on the Camera Position values (they probably read 220.0, 126.5) to open up the Camera Position settings dialog box.

56. In the Camera Position settings dialog box, set the Camera Position keyframe value for the X-axis to 275 and leave the Y-axis unchanged.

Make a RAM preview. If you like the way the camera moves, you're all done. If not, go back and tweak your settings. You can also try changing the shadow position or shadow color.

If you're happy with your project after looking at the RAM preview, it's time to render your final movie with all the correct settings for your appropriate output and/or distribution method. Now would also be a good time to save your project.

57. With the current Composition or Time Layout window as the active window, or with the Composition's name/icon selected in the Project window, go up to your menu bar and select Composition➡Make Movie.

58. A Save Movie As dialog box opens. Save the movie as Farmer John to your desired folder or directory.

59. The Render Queue opens next. Here you need to change the Render Settings from Current Settings to Best Settings.

60. Next, click on the underlined Output Module setting and change the output module to your choice of format (QuickTime Movie was used in this example). Check "Import into project when done" so you can quickly see your movie once it's finished rendering.

```
┌─────────────────────────────────────────────────────┐
│                 Output Module Settings                │
├─────────────────────────────────────────────────────┤
│  ┌ Composition "Landscape.ai" ──────────────────┐    │
│  │  Format: [ QuickTime Movie    ▼]  ☑ Import into project when done │
│  │                                                │    │
│  │  ☑ Video Output ──────────────────────────────┐    │
│  │  [Format Options...]                          │    │
│  │  Animation Compressor        Channels: [ RGB            ▼] │
│  │  Spatial Quality = Most (100)                 │    │
│  │                              Depth:  [ Millions of Colors ▼] │
│  │                              Color:  [ Premultiplied (With Black) ▼] │
│  │  ┌ Stretch ───────────────────────────────────┐  │
│  │  │         Width    Height                      │  │
│  │  │ Rendering at:  320  ×  240   ☑ Lock Aspect Ratio to (4:3) │
│  │  │ Stretch to: [320] × [240]  [Custom        ▼] │
│  │  │ Stretch %:        ×        Stretch Quality [High ▼] │
│  │  └──────────────────────────────────────────────┘  │
│  │  ┌ Crop ──────────────────────────────────────┐  │
│  │  │ T:[ 0 ] L:[ 0 ] B:[ 0 ] R:[ 0 ]  Final Size: 320 × 240 │
│  │  └──────────────────────────────────────────────┘  │
│  │  ┌ Audio Output ──────────────────────────────┐  │
│  │  │ [Format Options...]                        │  │
│  │  │ [44,100 Hz ▼]  [16 Bit ▼]  [Stereo ▼]      │  │
│  │  └──────────────────────────────────────────────┘  │
│  │                          [ Cancel ] [  OK  ]       │
│  └────────────────────────────────────────────────────┘
```

61. In the same Output Module Settings dialog box, click on the Format Options button in the Video Output section.

```
┌────────────────────────────────────────────────────┐
│  ☑ Video Output ───────────────────────────────────┐│
│  [Format Options...]                                ││
│  Animation Compressor        Channels: [ RGB      ▼]││
│  Spatial Quality = Most (100)                       ││
│                              Depth:  [ Millions of Colors ▼]││
│                              Color:  [ Premultiplied (With Black) ▼]││
│  ┌ Stretch ────────────────────────────────────────┐│
│  │         Width    Height                          ││
│  │ Rendering at:  320  ×  240  ☑ Lock Aspect Ratio to (4:3) ││
│  │ Stretch to: [320] × [240]  [Custom            ▼] ││
│  │ Stretch %:        ×        Stretch Quality [High ▼] ││
│  └───────────────────────────────────────────────────┘│
│  ┌ Crop ───────────────────────────────────────────┐│
│  │ T:[ 0 ] L:[ 0 ] B:[ 0 ] R:[ 0 ]  Final Size: 320 × 240 ││
│  └───────────────────────────────────────────────────┘│
└────────────────────────────────────────────────────┘
```

NOTE

For vector-based graphics, the Animation codec is a better choice than Sorenson. The Medium Quality setting produces decent results while cutting your file size in half.

62. The Compression Settings dialog box pops up. For this example, choose Animation and set the slider to Medium Quality. Click OK twice to get back to the Render Queue.

TIP

If you checked the "Import into project when done" checkbox in the Output Module, simply double-click on the movie icon in your Project window.

TIP

If you plan on sharing your project file with others, especially cross-platform, you need to add the .aep extension to your project name.

63. When the Render Queue is finally ready, click Render.

After the render is complete, play your movie to make sure it came out the way you expected. If all is well, save your final project as Multiplane Cartoon.

Index

License Agreement

By opening this package, you are agreeing to be bound by the following agreement:

You may not copy or redistribute the entire CD-ROM as a whole. Copying and redistribution of individual software programs on the CD-ROM is governed by terms set by individual copyright holders.

This software is sold as-is, without warranty of any kind, either expressed or implied, including but not limited to the implied warranties of merchantability and fitness for a particular purpose. Neither the publisher nor its dealers or distributors assumes any liability for any alleged or actual damages arising from the use of this program. (Some states do not allow for the exclusion of implied warranties, so the exclusion may not apply to you.)

> **NOTE**
>
> This CD-ROM uses long and mixed-case filenames requiring the use of a protected-mode CD-ROM driver.

Installation Instructions

Windows 95, Windows 98, Windows NT 4, Mac OS, and Windows 2000 Installation Instructions

1. Insert the CD-ROM into your CD-ROM drive.

2. From the Windows desktop, double-click the **My Computer** icon.

3. Double-click on the icon representing your CD-ROM drive.

4. Double-click on the icon named **start_here.htm** to view the CD interface.